NATIONAL LAMPOON®

BALLS!

by STEVE HOFSTETTER

NATIONAL LAMPOON ®

BALLS!

SPORTS

by STEVE HOFSTETTER

Published by National Lampoon Press

National Lampoon, Inc. • 8228 Sunset Boulevard • Los Angeles • CA 90046 • USA

AMEX:NLN

NATIONAL LAMPOON, NATIONAL LAMPOON PRESS and colophon are trademarks of National Lampoon

National lampoon, Balls! an in your face look at sports
/ by Steve Hofstetter -- 1st ed.

p. cm.

ISBN-10: 0978832353
ISBN-13: 978-0978832353 – $12.95 U.S. – $15.95 Canada

Book Design and Production by
JK NAUGHTON

Cover by
Sam McCay

PRINTED IN THE UNITED STATES OF AMERICA

1   3   5   7   9   10   8   6   4   2

SEPTEMBER 2007

WWW.NATIONALLAMPOON.COM

The critics love Steve Hofstetter (and his Balls!)

Steve Hofstetter is one of the bright, young minds in comedy. He has a unique take on life that always brings a smile to your face.
Paul Fichtenbaum, Managing Editor
SportsIllustrated.com

Funny sh**.
Adam Duritz, Counting Crows

This book is more fun than a Rally Monkey with a cup full of change at ten cent beer night!
Norm Wamer, WLQR AM 1470
Toledo, OH

I'm providing an endorsement for this book in exchange for Steve Hofstetter doing yard work. He's better at writing than mowing.
Jim Gaffigan, comedian

Steve Hofstetter's sports comedy is like regular comedy on steroids.
Dale Jones, KVSA AM 1220
McGehee AR

If I ever read a book,
it will definitely be this one.
Comedian Jeffrey Ross

I love Steve Hofstetter more than I love canned
pears... And I friggin love canned pears.
Comedian Mitch Fatel

That is one funny redhead.
Garrett Morris
original cast member of
Saturday Night Live

Steve – There's only room for one red headed
comic in this business.
And his name is Carrot Top.
Comedian Bill Burr

Hilarious, whip smart, thin and young...if I didn't
adore Steve Hofstetter so damn much, I'd really
have to hate him.
TV and Radio Personality Frank DeCaro

It's great to know there are good humor
columnists out there.
Mary Jane Wilkinson
Boston Globe

*Dedicated to Kelly, who loves me
enough to try to love sports, too.*

Acknowledgements:

Thanks to Scott Rubin, Zach Posner, Marcy Goot, Michael Klein, Dan Laikin, Bruce Long, Jay Naughton and everyone else at National Lampoon for bringing the championship back. Shari Gibbons and Lisa Jones Johnson for putting me in the game. Chris Edling for being my super-sub off the bench. Ben Feigin, Kate Magill, and Steve Landau for their coaching. Paul Fichtenbaum, Jimmy Traina, Bobby Clay and *Sports Illustrated* for letting me trash-talk. Rich Libero and NHL.com for letting me trash-talk more. Patty LaDuca, Vinny Mallozzi, and the *New York Times* for the post-game interview. Stephanie Geosits, Neil Schwartz, Joe Perello, Mark Mandrake, and Yankees Xtreme for helping me make it to the show. Ryan Murphy, Chris Strait, Rich Ragains, Keith Alberstadt, Cody Marley, Elliot Steingart, Adam Hunter, Jason Weichelt, Tre Giles, Eugene Chin, and everyone who built the *Sports Minute (Or So)* into a contender. My boys at Collegehumor.com for always believing, even during rebuilding years. Mike Allen, Dave Andrews, Eddie Brill, Peter Case, Jon Chattman, Shelly Cobb, Chris Colston, Rick Duck, Tim Ellis, Paul Fichtenbaum, Francene, Jim Gaffigan, Shane Gesundheit, Dave Harrison, Nadine Haobsch, Maz Jobrani, Dale Jones, Cory Kopsa, Greg Mislak, Phil Parker, Dave Richards, Buddy Rizer, Jeffrey Ross, Jon Scher, Julie Seabaugh, Doug Sheckler, Norm Wamer, and Charlie Weston for the post game coverage. Denis Donohue and the 1986 World Champion New York Mets for representing Queens. Of course my brother Adam and my father Marty, who taught me to play (and wish the Dodgers were still in Brooklyn). And Gets by Buckner, Matteau! Matteau!, Wide Right, Posterizing, and all the moments that made each of us sports fans. – Steve Hofstetter

www.stevehofstetter.com

Table of Contents

CHAPTER ZERO:
FAQ 17

CHAPTER ONE:
Baseball: Steroids – Not Just For Kids Anymore! 19

CHAPTER TWO:
Basketball: At Least the Last Two Minutes Matter 37

CHAPTER THREE:
Football: The Longest GM Ad in History 53

CHAPTER FOUR:
Hockey: Yes, It's Still a Sport 75

CHAPTER FIVE:
Soccer, Golf, and Other Sports That Don't
Deserve Their Own Chapters 87

CHAPTER SIX:
College Sports: The Paid Athletes of
Tomorrow Getting Paid Today 113

CHAPTER SEVEN:
Fame: Someone Tell Shaquille O'Neal to
Stop Rapping 123

CHAPTER EIGHT:
Fan is Short for Fanatic, Which is Short For
Fanatical Nutcase 131

CHAPTER NINE:
Ruthian Players, Like Babe Ruth 149

CHAPTER TEN:
The People Who Suck, And the Women
Who Love Them 187

CHAPTER ELEVEN:
Why Do Hot Dogs Cost Four Dollars?
(Get it? It's called Chapter Eleven.) 207

CHAPTER TWELVE:
What Comes Next? (Just Bust a Move) 211

CHAPTER ZERO

1) Will this book teach me about sports?

If you've bought this book to learn more about sports, you've bought the wrong book. If you've picked up this book with the intention of buying it to learn about sports, yes, that's exactly what will happen when you read it. That person at the register will help you complete your purchase.

2) What's the point of this book?

This book will actually teach you a bit about sports. Mainly that sports are funny. Where else can a grown man play a children's game in a jumpsuit for a million dollars and complain that he's not getting paid enough? That's comedy, no matter how you slice it. And don't slice this book, that will make it hard to read.

3) Who is this book for?

This book is for the fan that appreciates sports for what they are – a fun diversion from an otherwise mundane existence. If that's you, welcome aboard. If that's not, thanks for the $30. Or whatever bargain price they're selling this for. It's really worth $30.

4) Should this book be taken seriously?

No, never. This book is about sports. And sports should never be taken too seriously. Some of you will get offended that I mock your favorite team or player, and you should get over it. I'm kidding. Also, your favorite team sucks. They all do. Even the ones that win suck eventually. Hell, look at the Cardinals this year. (Note: if you're reading this book in a few years and the Cardinals are good, replace them with whoever is eating it this year.)

5) Are you done yet?

Yes. So pick up a hot dog and sit down for a few innings or periods or quarters or laps or frames or rounds or whatever your sport calls them. And don't get mad if I got something wrong. I got most of this stuff off the internet.

CHAPTER ONE

Baseball: Steroids – Not Just For Kids Anymore!

Beginnings

In 1839, Abner Doubleday invented baseball in a cow pasture in Cooperstown, New York. What was so amazing about Doubleday's invention was that he was nowhere near Cooperstown that year and we also have records of baseball being played in Massachusetts as early as 1792. Thus Doubleday is almost as amazing as George Washington or Abraham Lincoln, who have the uncanny ability to make their birthdays fall on Mondays every year. Just two years after Doubleday invented baseball, Al Gore invented the Internet.

The person responsible for the Doubleday myth is Abner Graves, a man who would later murder his wife and end up in an institution for the criminally insane. Even if he wasn't a crazy wife-murderer, Graves was also just five years old in 1839, making him the least credible source not named Kato Kaelin. But Doubleday is a war hero, so his story is easily digestible for the average American and perfect for Fox News.

The real lesson here is that in the early 1800s, everyone in America was named Abner.

Doubleday's great-great-grand nephew, Nelson Doubleday, Jr., eventually bought the Mets, which explains a lot.

Other Things Abner Doubleday Invented

Sliced Bread

The Steam Engine

Astroturf

Decaffeinated Coffee

Calculus

Obstetric Ultrasound Imaging

The Bedazzler

Real Beginnings

The current theory is that the real father of baseball was Alexander Joy Cartwright. Unlike Sean Kemp, who is the father of basketball. Cartwright was both the first to write down the rules of baseball and the manliest guy to ever be named "Joy."

Cartwright's team was called "The New York Knicker-bockers," named for his firefighting brigade and a crappy basketball team. It turns out the only reason Cartwright wrote down the rules is that he was forced to; in order to rent the field, he had to form an official club which required official rules. So really the father of baseball is money.

Because of baseball's separate regional evolutions, the mid-19th century saw two versions developing: The New York Game and The Massachusetts Game. The New York

Game of baseball eventually finished ahead, which is no surprise to Red Sox fans.

The First Leagues

The first league was the National Association of Base Ball Players, comprised of over 400 teams of players named Abner. Soon after came the National Association of Professional Base Ball Players, and the National League of Professional Base Ball Clubs, which was known for its utter inability to win an all-star game. Competing leagues sprung up, including leagues like the Players League, the Western League, the Pacific Coast League, the Eastern League, and the Justice League.

Rejected Names For Other Leagues

National Association of Base Ball Players Who Are Associated Nationally

Professional Professionals Who Play Baseball Professionally

American National Professional Association of American Nationals (Of Baseball)

The WNBA

Goodbye, Other Leagues

Most leagues posed no threat to the National League, as the National League controlled most of the major cities. In 1894, the Western League began play in a few major cities, but mostly places like Grand Rapids, Sioux City, and Toledo. Back then, Ohio must have been considered Western.

Within a few years, the Western League went on the attack, changing its name to the American League, moving franchises to bigger cities, and instituting the Designated Hitter. The two major leagues then started bidding for players, and the other leagues basically gave up and formed an association themselves. There were now three entities – the National League, the America League, and the National Association of Professional Baseball Leagues. You've never heard of the NAPBL because they don't really matter.

The structure became simple – the NL and AL would be two friendly leagues, playing each other in a "World Series" where teams would compete from places all over the world, like Ohio. The NAPBL's job was to sell contracts to the NL and AL. And all three organizations would prevent their players from choosing who they played for or making any significant amount of money. Everybody wins!

The Dead Ball Era

1900-1919 is commonly known as the Dead Ball Era, mainly because steroids weren't invented yet. The era was also known for dominant pitchers like Cy Young, who won the Cy Young award every year. That was despite the emergence of a young Roger Clemens.

In 1901, baseball's average attendance was 3,247 – only slightly higher than a Royals game today. But the first few years of the century saw a surge in popularity. Attendance almost doubled by 1909, giving rise to new stadiums that would eventually be named for banks.

The Dead Ball Era also featured Ty "Georgia Peach" Cobb, the first professional athlete who was also a professional dillhole. While The Peach would be followed in sports by legendary dillholes like Bill Romanowski, Mike Tyson, and Barry Bonds, Cobb was truly a pioneer in dillholeness.

In 1919, the Black Sox scandal became one of baseball's most formative incidents, when Shoeless Joe Jackson showed up to a game wearing black socks after labor day. Also, his White Sox threw the World Series because their cheapskate owner didn't pay them enough. Jackson and his teammates were shamed, and received lifetime bans that are inexplicably still in place long after they died. The Black Sox scandal led to Major League Baseball's harsh stance on gambling, and launched the career of actor D.B. Sweeney.

Bring On The Dingers

In 1920, a rule change prevented pitchers from scuffing baseballs. After Ray Chapman was killed when he was hit by a hard-to-see pitch that year, umpires actually started enforcing the rule. They wanted to prevent anyone else from dying, and also chicks dig the long ball.

The easier-to-see baseballs were also easier to hit, and it didn't hurt that Babe Ruth was one of the guys hitting them. Ruth had been sold to the Yankees after the 1919 season along with Bostons' chances of winning a World Series for the next eight decades. That year Ruth hit a then record 54 home runs, which would have sounded more impressive if this book were written in the 1990s.

Other stars of the era included Jimmie Foxx, Hack Wilson, and Lou Gehrig (who eventually died of Jimmie Foxx Disease). Also rising to prominence was Hank Greenberg, one of the first in a long line of at least seven good Jewish athletes.

The 1920s and 1930s saw the introduction of traditions like radio broadcasts, the All-Star Game, and the Hall of Fame. The first class elected to the Hall included Ty Cobb, Walter

Johnson, Christy Mathewson, Babe Ruth, and Honus Wagner. Pete Rose was left off the ballot.

You Let Who Play Baseball?

1941 was a huge year for baseball. Ted Williams hit .400, Joe DiMaggio hit in 56 consecutive games, and Ty Cobb probably hit someone for bringing him the wrong kind of coffee. But soon after, baseball was affected deeply by World War II. Remember, this was before famous people were completely above the law.

Many players left to serve America, giving rise to The All-American Girls Professional Baseball League. The AAGPBL was not just a distraction – it was enough of a success to last eleven seasons, partially because of America's infatuation with Madonna. One of the teams was called "The Milwaukee Chicks," which would be a great nickname for the Brewers.

If women playing baseball wasn't enough to freak out America's average sexist bigot (read: Ty Cobb), 1947 saw the de-segregation of baseball. Players like Jackie Robinson, Larry Doby, and Lando Calrissian all helped their teams to win pennants and be much less afraid of black people.

Who Can't Play Major League Baseball Today?

Parrots	Mountains
Camels	Paraplegics
Babies	Women
Dead People	

Westward Ho

From 1903 to 1953, no major league team moved cities. But when the Boston Braves left for Milwaukee and set attendance records, many teams followed their strategy. It was perfect: move to a new city where the fans will be energized for a few years before getting bored again. The Browns soon moved to Baltimore and the Athletics soon moved to Kansas City. The moves worked so well that the Braves and the Athletics moved again shortly thereafter. The Braves' second move marked the last time anyone ever willingly attended a baseball game in Milwaukee.

After the 1957 season, both the Giants and Dodgers left New York for California, mainly to tear my poor father's heart out. Also, the west had obvious allure to an owner. San Francisco fans were known for their toleration of steroid use, and Los Angeles was a great place to watch three innings of quality baseball. California would eventually have five teams, since the Padres technically count as a team.

The Steroid-Free Home Run Race

1961 saw the most historic season in baseball history, as Yankee teammates Roger Maris and Mickey Mantle raced each other to break Babe Ruth's record for home runs in a single season. Roger Maris, who looked eerily like actor Barry Pepper, won out despite enduring season long chants of "A-Rod Sucks." Maris won the MVP in his first and second seasons with the club, set the home run record, and saved the 1962 World Series with a phenomenal play in right field. Yankee fans hated him anyway because, hey, that's what they do.

Expansion

In 1961, baseball added the Los Angeles Angels, who later became the California Angels, the Anaheim Angels, the Los Angeles Angels of Anaheim, and the Green Bay Packers. Since the Washington Senators had moved to Minnesota, 1961 also saw the rebirth of the Washington Senators with a new franchise. That team moved to Texas a few years later. Today there's another team in Washington, and I look forward to finding out where they're going to move.

In 1962, baseball added the New York Mets and the Houston Colt 45s. Really, that was the Astros' name back then. The Mets quickly became the losingest team in baseball history, and the Colt 45s quickly adopted Billy Dee Williams as their spokesman. By the end of the 1960s, Major League Baseball also added the Kansas City Royals, the Seattle Pilots, the Montreal Expos, and the San Diego Padres, who have combined for 17 wins since. Baseball didn't expand again until the 1990s, when they added the Colorado Rockies, Florida Marlins, Arizona Diamondbacks, and Tampa Bay Embarrassment To The League.

Hard To Trust Something Called Anti-Trust

Due to an anti-trust exemption granted in 1922, Major League Baseball has the unique power to control commerce over state lines. What that means to anyone who does not wear a judge's robe is that MLB can determine who buys and sells their teams, and where those teams go. In other words, when MLB let Peter Magowan buy the Giants in 1993 for $15 million less than Vince Piazza so they wouldn't be moved to Florida, it was pretty crappy. Though it turned out well for Piazza, since no one in Florida will pay to see a baseball game.

Where Else Can Baseball Expand?

New Orleans
Pro: Great stadium music.
Con: Players constantly taking off jerseys in exchange for beads.

Atlantic City
Pro: Pete Rose available for extra BP.
Con: Pete Rose available for extra BP.

Paris
Pro: Jerry Lewis singing the national anthem.
Con: Whenever the team gets down by more than three runs, they surrender.

Salt Lake City
Pro: Sports are the only fun thing in the entire state.
Con: Bringing the wives on road trips gets expensive.

Brooklyn
Pro: Games against the San Francisco Jints.
Con: Alternate side of the street parking in players' parking lot.

Bejing
Pro: Communism helps maintain competitive balance.
Con: Rally panda?

Havana
Pro: Tons of good prospects to choose from.
Con: One of them is named "Fidel."

New Jersey
Pro: Springstein concerts.
Con: Fuggeddaboudit.

Des Moines
Pro: Shoeless Joe shows up for Old Timers Day.
Con: Great farm system, but terrible minor leagues.

Who Wants To See Good Pitching Anyway?

In 1968, pitching dominated baseball. St. Louis' Bob Gibson led the league with a 1.12 ERA and Detroit's Denny McLain won 31 games. Amazingly, that's more games than the Tigers won in the 1990s. But because chicks still dig the long ball, three major rule changes were instituted. One, the pitcher's mound was lowered. Two, the strike zone was reduced. Three, the designated hitter was added. Most baseball fans were thrilled about that last one; before the DH, we hardly got a chance to see aging malcontents with bad knees.

Other Suggested Rule Changes to Increase Scoring

Strike out a hitter, do a shot. (The David Wells Rule)

One ball walks. (The John Kruk Rule)

Hit this sign, win a suit: a paternity suit. (The Chipper Jones Rule)

Fattest player always plays in center. (The Other David Wells Rule)

Free Agency is Not Free

In 1970, *Flood v. Major League Baseball* changed the game forever. It turns out Flood had rebroadcast a game without express written consent, and also he wanted to be a free agent. The problem was that the term "free agent" wouldn't be coined for another five years, so Flood lost his case. The Flood case did eventually lead to free agency, which led to twenty-five million dollar salaries, which led to four dollar hot dogs. So, thanks Curt. Seriously, thanks.

Now that teams had the ability to sign whomever they wanted, the Yankees suddenly got good again.

The Swinging Seventies

The Oakland A's and Cincinnati Reds dominated the 1970s, but no one cares about them today so I'll gloss over that. The big news of the Seventies was that Hank Aaron broke Babe Ruth's career home run record with 755 home runs. That record still stands today, unless you're reading this after Barry Bonds broke it.

Ch-Ch-Changes

Before the 1980s, pitch counts did not exist, and thus neither did middle relievers. Most pitchers pitched the whole game on three days rest and walked twenty miles to school in a snowstorm and liked it. But now that coaches were counting pitches, pitchers suddenly believed that they needed five days rest to throw six innings. This practice is even more extreme today. At the current rate of deterioration, starting pitchers in 2020 will be removed halfway through the second inning.

Another change was the science of weight training. Players now worked out with personal trainers on advanced machines in elaborate weight rooms. Then, they took steroids.

Of course, the biggest change for baseball was television. While regional coverage had existed for years, cable networks like TBS and shows like Game of the Week finally gave fans an opportunity to see teams across the country in cities like New York, Atlanta, New York, Atlanta, and New York.

Baseball Players Are Better Than You

As sponsorship dollars rolled in and the memorabilia markets took off, baseball salaries rose and rose. Dave Winfield set records in 1981 by signing a ten-year, twenty-three million dollar contract. Twenty years later, John Rocker made that much money every time he used the N-word.

Money dominated baseball in the 1990s, allowing free-spending owners like Florida's Wayne Huizenga to buy championships. The Marlins won the World Series in their fifth year – though by the time they reached the White House that off-season, only 11 of their champs were left in uniform. True to his corporate history, the Blockbuster Video owning Huizenga rented a winning team and gave it back a few days later.

1994 also saw the first cancellation of the World Series, after players and owners couldn't agree as to whether Miller Lite tasted great or was less filling. Many fans blamed acting commissioner Bud Selig's do-nothing regime for the rift. Owners, of course, promoted Selig a few years later. Selig would later end the All-Star Game in a tie, approve selling ads on bases, and announce he was contracting two teams the day after the World Series. Eventually, Selig won fans back with an even bigger announcement – he's retiring.

> **Bombshells Bud Selig Will Reveal Before He Retires**
>
> "I ran over the rally monkey."
>
> "I'm contracting the third inning."
>
> "My new toupee is made from the San Diego Chicken."
>
> "Uniforms will now have built-in green screens to accommodate our advertising contract with Fox."
>
> "I'm slowly building a team of cryogenically frozen all-stars."
>
> "Next season, fans across the world will get to vote for the most memorable moment of 1987."
>
> "I'm on steroids."

Hulk Smash!

In 1998, Sammy Sosa and Mark McGwire raced for the home run record much like Mantle and Maris did in 1961. The only difference was that Mantle and Maris weren't created by a mad scientist. Mark McGwire has since addressed questions of steroid use with all the honesty of Ollie North, and Sammy Sosa sneezed his way onto the disabled list. There's no proof yet either one was on steroids, but, yeah, they were both on steroids.

Many have admitted to drugging since that season, including Jose Canseco, Ken Caminiti, and Kate Moss. Most recently, Major League Baseball has begun suspending players that test positive for steroids, a departure from their previous policy of saying, "shhhhh." The biggest suspension thus far was Rafael Palmiero, who thankfully lost his creepy endorsement deal with Viagra.

The proliferation of steroids has also called many of the game's recent records into question, including single-season home runs (Barry Bonds), single-season slugging percentage (Barry Bonds), and single-season hat size (Barry Bonds).

True Fake Stat: 14

Viagra Rafael Palmiero had to take before it was considered a steroid.

Good Things Come in Small Markets, Except Good Baseball Teams

One major problem caused by free agency is the lack of competitive balance between the Yankees and teams that are not the Yankees. Teams in smaller markets like Pittsburgh, Kansas City, and Montreal can't hope to compete with much richer teams, or at least that's their excuse. The Expos were so bad that they became the first team to move in thirty years, preferring instead to lose their ballgames in Washington DC.

Teams in Minnesota and Oakland have been managed well, but have a much harder time attracting free agents, and not just because they're awful places to live. Teams like the New York Yankees, Boston Red Sox, and the Atlanta Braves can afford to pay more, and thus are perennial contenders. Teams like the Los Angeles Dodgers can also afford to pay more, but often remain crappy due to horrid mismanagement.

How The Cleveland Indians Woo Players

"We heard you can whistle, so we're having you inducted into the Rock and Roll Hall of Fame."

"We're going to replace Jacobs field with one of those new nostalgic stadiums."

"Drew Carey agreed to carry your bag on road trips."

"You'll be one of the top ten football players in the city!"

"Three words: free drink refills."

"Our city nickname may not be pretty, but at least it rhymes."

"We're not the Royals."

"Don't like Cleveland? No problem. We'll just pick up and move to Baltimore."

The Stinking Rich Get Stinking Richer

The New York Yankees established YES Network in 1999 as a loophole to sign more free agents away from small teams. Since YES is technically owned by the parent company of the Yankees but not considered part of the team itself, the Yankees do not have to pay luxury tax on anything earned by the network. In other words, we're getting hosed. The rival Boston Red Sox have NESN, whose relationship to YES is much like the Red Sox to the Yankees. NESN has been around longer than YES, but isn't near as profitable and has won fewer World Championships.

Strike One

The owners and players have been fighting ever since baseball started. The first fight was back in 1912, when the players threw all the owners' tea into Boston Harbor. But it wasn't until 1981 that the newly unionized players actually struck. While pre-season strikes and lockouts were fairly common in the 1970s, 1981 saw the loss of seven weeks in the middle of the season and the only chance the Brewers ever had. The main reason for the strike was a protest of the owners' increased compensation for the loss of a free agent. Most fans sided with the players, as no restaurant is compensated when their best waiter leaves for a better job.

Strike Two

In 1994, a second strike damaged the fans' respect for both owners AND players, as the root of the strike was revenue sharing. The owners made an offer that they claimed would raise average salaries from $1.2 million to $2.6 million in seven years, as long as they got a salary cap. The Players Union wanted to prevent the cap, as well as get custody of the kids and the weekend house in Cabo. The fans just wanted to see baseball. After the cancellation of the 1994 World Series and a few weeks of the 1995 season, fans finally realized that baseball is, at its very heart, a business. And Bud Selig and Donald Fehr, at their hearts, don't have any.

Suggestions For MLB's Collective Bargaining Agreement

All teams that receive luxury tax benefits must use part of the proceeds to purchase Baltic Avenue.

Steroid testing consists of more than just asking players, "Hey man, are you on steroids?"

Karl Marx to oversee new revenue sharing program.

If your team is down by ten or more runs, all stadium concessions are half price.*

Starting pitchers must be removed via oversized hook and a loud cry of "yoink!"

Pete Rose banned from crappy Maaco commercials.

Milwaukee Brewers games consist of one inning of play and eight innings of sausage race.

Darryl Strawberry limited to just five more second chances.

In an effort to speed up the games, the ceremonial first pitch now counts.

Players who say "it's not about the money" must play for free for the next week.

Any game tied after the eleventh will be settled by a spirited game of "Rock, Paper, Scissors."

*Void in Colorado

These Poor, Poor Millionaires

Recently, players and owners seem to be getting along better. Before the 2007 season, they agreed to a new five year labor deal that includes a minimum salary of $400,000. Fans have a similar contract, where they're guaranteed at least $5.15 an hour.

Fans that are upset with their favorite players and teams, however, should think about how they complain. Most do so while wearing a jersey and watching their club on Direct TV. If you don't like how much this stuff costs, stop being the guy that pays for it. Baseball is a business, and it always will be. When your bank raises its rates beyond what's reasonable, you leave for another bank – might I suggest you do the same when your stadium is named for one.

Why I'd Rather Watch the Little League World Series Than Major League Baseball

When little leaguers age during an off-season, it's only by 2-3 years.

If the game ends in a tie, at least both sides get ice cream.

DUIs are much less common.

Performance enhancers consist of chocolate bars and Jolt Cola.

Florida fans have something to cheer about.

The commissioner actually works in his office.

No one even half the size of Rich Garces.

CHAPTER TWO

Basketball: At Least the Last Two Minutes Matter

Beginnings

Fortunately, we actually know who invented basketball. Unfortunately, it was a gym teacher at a YMCA. The only way to make that story lamer is if it happened while he was listening to Kenny G.

In 1891, Dr. James Naismith was trying to find something to occupy the students at what would become Springfield College. Naismith developed an indoor game where players would toss a soccer ball into a peach basket. A peach basket? Look at that, it somehow got lamer. Impressive.

Anyway, since the ball had to be thrown upwards, it was not too rough to be played indoors – which was necessary due to the harsh winter. So if Naismith had been teaching in Florida, we'd all be watching The National Shuffleboard League.

The original baskets had bottoms, requiring a long poking stick to be used after each basket. So the game wasn't quite as exciting back then. But poking stick and all, basketball spread quickly through YMCAs, High Schools, and 125th street. A decade later, play had gotten a little rougher and the YMCA actually started discouraging the game. Good call guys – basketball really hasn't done well since then.

The early game was very different than the one we know today, featuring lopsided brown balls, no dribbling, and very few players named Shaquille.

True Fake Stat: 0

Chicks James Naismith was banging at the time he invented basketball.

The College Game

Unlike baseball where players don't ever go to college, basketball wouldn't be nearly as popular if it weren't for the college game. By 1910, schools like Columbia University, the University of Chicago, and the US Naval Academy all had teams. Some good teams started back then, too. Basketball had grown very popular, but was getting so rough that President Theodore Roosevelt suggested that college basketball form a governing body. He also suggested that governing body be called "Roosevelt's Rapscallions," and that they'd ride together through the countryside defending basketball's honor.

Roosevelt's suggestion spurred the creation of the Intercollegiate Athletic Association, which eventually became the National Collegiate Athletic Association (more commonly known as the NAACP). The NCAA now oversees many college sports and determines which college athletes are allowed to get paid.

Ladies First

Women's basketball actually spread before men's basketball, because men were to busy having real jobs. The first college team was at the all female Smith College in 1892, just a year after the game was invented. Naismith's rules were modified, however, to allow women to retain their femininity while playing the game. That's still true today – when I think women's basketball, I think femininity.

By 1895, women had teams at Mount Holyoke, Vassar, and Bryn Mawr. All-girls schools were perfect for basketball, as the lack of men created a need for physical activity. And lesbians. In 1896, the Stanford women beat the University of California women in a 9 on 9 game, with a final score of 2-1. Thankfully women's games are much more high-scoring now, with at least 7 points per team.

"Professional" Basketball

By the 1920s, hundreds of paid teams cropped up around the country, featuring games in armories, dance halls, and broom closets. Leagues opened and closed like they were a woman dating Wilt Chaimberlain, and there was not much structure to the men's game. The most successful teams were barnstorming clubs like the New York Renaissance Five (The Rens) and the Harlem Globetrotters. Both teams were all black, much like the NBA today. Except Utah.

The women, on the other hand, had structure. In 1905, the National Women's Basketball Committee's Executive Committee on Basket Ball Rules was established. Really, that's true. The Committee put together strict rules, including having eleven officials but only nine players. Really, that's true. These rules were later published in paperback by Ellen and Sherrie and simply called "The Rules." See, there, I'm kidding. Maybe.

My Team is Better Than Your Team

Women again got to things more quickly than the men, which is the opposite of real life. The first women's national championship was established in 1926, 12 years ahead of the men. Women reading this, however, can't take too much pride in their early start as some of the teams competing in said championships had names like "The All American Red Heads Team." I'm a redhead and even I know that's absurd.

Men, in the meantime, finally organized a championship in 1938, when the National Invitation Tournament was held in New York. The NCAA Tournament started a year later, but the NIT actually remained the respected championship for the next two decades. Odd, since winning the NIT now is college basketball's equivalent of winning the Special Olympics. The NIT was eventually bought by the NCAA, and now serves as a way to make all the losing teams feel less like losers. That's right, you're all special.

Once national championships were established, fans had a chance to root for their team in a more structured environment, as well as the opportunity to lose their office pool to a secretary who has never watched basketball.

College Basketball Today

Now that you have the basic history, I'll discuss college basketball more in the chapter about college sports. That's what it's there for, genius.

Putting the High Back In High School

Thanks in no small part to its low cost and small roster size, basketball thrived in American high schools. High school basketball remains equally as popular today, as the largest high school sport and a great way for parents to live out their unrealized dreams through their children. The National Federation of State High School Associations reports that there are currently over one million high school basketball players, most of which live in Indiana.

The NBA: Freaking Finally

In 1946, just fifty-five years after the rest of the world started playing basketball, a professional association was finally born. Major League Baseball was already working on integration by the time the NBA was working on Game One.

Actually, the league wasn't even the NBA yet. For the first three years, it was called the Basketball Association of

America, or the BAA. The first game was between the New York Knickerbockers and the Toronto Huskies, which would be a good name for a WNBA team. Pretty soon, people realized that calling a league "BAA" was almost as dumb as having a team called the Huskies, and the NBA was born.

The BAA merged with the National Basketball League in 1949 to become the NBA. Beginning with 17 teams, the league contracted into eight teams soon after, and all eight still stand today. The Knicks stand in one place while their opponents dribble around them, but they stand.

Bigger Means Better

With consolidation came movement, as many teams moved to big cities in order to attract more fans. As if Rochester, Syracuse, Moline, and Fort Wayne aren't big cities.

The Atlanta Hawks were known as the Blackhawks and played in what is now known as the Quad Cities – an area consisting of Moline, Rock Island, Bettendorf, and Davenport. Oddly enough, that sprawling metropolis couldn't support an NBA team. The Tri-City Blackhawks became the Milwaukee Hawks in 1951, then the St. Louis Hawks, and finally the Atlanta Braves.

The Sacramento Kings began as the Rochester Royals, a team that was probably better at baseball than the Kansas City Royals. The name was derived from sponsor Crown Royal Whiskey, a drink that now helps fans stomach the Kansas City Royals. Anyway, the Royals moved to Cincinnati in 1957 and Kansas City in 1972, where they were confusingly renamed the Kings. Despite using the name Royals a full twenty-five years before the baseball team, the basketball

Royals still had to change their name when they got to KC. The Kansas City Kings eventually moved to Sacramento, where they have enjoyed the weather and their ability to never win a championship.

Over in Indiana, the Ft. Wayne Pistons got tired of a city that made them play in a high school gym (really, that's where they started) and moved to Detroit in 1957. Luckily, Detroit is known for manufacturing cars, so no one thought the name "Pistons" was weird.

And in 1962, the Philadelphia Warriors moved to San Francisco to become the Golden State Warriors. The Syracuse Nationals replaced them in Philadelphia, changing their name to the 76ers, in honor of how many shots Allen Iverson would eventually take per game.

Along with the New York Knicks, the Minneapolis Lakers, and the Boston Celtics, every NBA team was now playing in a major city. Syracuse, Rochester, Fort Wayne, and Moline, however, got to watch some really good high school ball. I think some of those high school teams moved, too.

True Fake Stat: 7

Combined things to do in Syracuse, Rochester, Fort Wayne, and Moline.

Color Barrier? Really?

When the NBA started, almost all the players were white. The Knicks technically had a Japanese player in 1947 when the 5'7" Wataru Misaka suited up in the tiniest little uniform you ever saw. The Japanese continue to dominate basketball today, at least on the video game side of things.

Black players started playing in the league in 1950 with the addition of Chuck Cooper, Nat "Sweetwater" Clifton, Earl Lloyd, and Lando Calrissian. Today there are two or three more.

Big Moments in NBA Color Barrier History

1947: Wataru Misaka becomes the first ethnic minority to play in the BAA.

1950: Several NBA teams add black players.

1966: Bill Russell becomes the first black head coach.

2008: The overwhelming majority of NBA players are black.

2134: The NBA has its first black owner.

The Minneapolis Dynasty

When the Professional Basketball League of America folded, its players were distributed in a dispersal draft, and the Minneapolis Lakers got George Mikan. Mikan led the Lakers to the NBL Championship in 1948, the BAA championship in 1949, and the NBA championship in 1950, 1952, 1953, and 1954. In fairness, there were hardly any teams back then.

The indoor game thrived in Minneapolis, as it's the coldest city in America and no one wants to go outside. Other indoor sports in Minneapolis that do well include domed baseball, ice hockey, and repeatedly watching "Fargo."

The Boston Dynasty and The Los Angeles Semi-Dynasty

In 1956, the Boston Celtics traded for the rights to draft Bill Russell, who teamed with Bob Cousy and coach Red Auerbach to give the franchise eleven titles in thirteen years – including eight in a row. The Celtics were so dominant that the Minneapolis Lakers moved to Los Angeles just to get a fresh start. The Celtics beat the Los Angeles Lakers in the NBA finals six times in eight years, which is even more amazing when you consider how bad the Celtics are now.

The Lakers finally beat the Celtics in the finals in the 1980s. I'd be impressed if the Lakers hadn't already lost to them six times in eight years. The Lakers' franchise, in the meantime, has lost the NBA finals a record 14 times, which is amazing considering some franchises haven't even been around for that many seasons.

The ABA and the Addition of Funk

The NBA seems to take forever to institute positive changes, not even having a shot clock before 1954. So an upstart league was just the thing to force the NBA to actually get interesting. In 1967, the American Basketball Association formed and began raiding the NBA for talent. Leading scorer Rick Barry jumped ship and took his underhanded free throws with him. He shot underhand? What a wiener.

The ABA also allowed the signing of players who hadn't yet graduated college, including stars like Julius Erving and LeBron James. Erving and his tomahawk dunk kept the fledgling league alive until 1976, when his New York Nets joined the NBA along with the Indiana Pacers, San Antonio Spurs, and Denver Nuggets. Also joining were some rule changes, like including the three-point line and the slam dunk contest. These two additions made basketball somewhat tolerable for generations to come.

Which Are ABA Teams?

See if you can tell the difference between actual ABA teams and ones I made up.

Anaheim Amigos

Baltimore Claws

Carolina Cougars

Dallas Chaparrals

Denver Rockets

Houston Mavericks

Kentucky Colonels

Los Angeles Stars

Memphis Pros

Memphis Tams

Miami Floridians

Minnesota Muskies

New Jersey Americans

New Orleans Buccaneers

New York Nets

Oakland Oaks

Pittsburgh Condors

Pittsburgh Pipers

San Diego Conquistadors

San Diego Sails

Utah Stars

Virginia Squires

Washington Capitols

Answer: They're all real, because that league was ridiculous. The Chaparrals? Wow.

Expanding, Expanding, Expanding

To combat the ABA, the NBA started expanding to major cities. Before 1967, the NBA had added just two teams. 1961 saw the addition of the Chicago Packers, who later became the Chicago Zephyrs, Baltimore Bullets, Capital Bullets, Washington Bullets, Washington Wizards, and Los Angeles Angels of Anaheim. In 1966, the league tried Chicago again, this time with the Chicago Bulls. The name thankfully stuck.

But in the nine years that the ABA threatened NBA supremacy, the NBA added eight teams to counteract the upstart league. The ABA-influenced expansion saw the birth of the Seattle Supersonics, the Milwaukee Bucks, Phoenix Suns, Portland Trail Blazers, and Cleveland Cavaliers. The league also added The Los Angeles Clippers, the Houston Rockets, and the Utah Jazz but called them silly things and made them play in different cities. Actually, two of the three played briefly in San Diego, a city that also couldn't keep either of its ABA teams afloat. Note: San Diego hates basketball.

In 1980, the league expanded to include the Dallas Mavericks. 1988 saw the addition of the Charlotte Hornets and Miami Heat, and with 1989 came the Minnesota Timberwolves and the Orlando Magic. And 1996 saw the addition of the Toronto Raptors and Vancouver Grizzlies, which was the league's apology for adding two teams without an "S" at the end of their names. Seriously, the Heat and the Magic? What's wrong with Florida?

Finally in 2003, the league added a team in Charlotte for a second time, just a year after the Hornets ran away to New Orleans since Charlotte couldn't support an NBA franchise. Brilliant move. The league may as well go back to no shot clock and white players.

At this rate, there'll be 752 NBA teams by 2012, with at least one located in every major city. Except San Diego.

Where Else Can The NBA Expand?

Fort Wayne

Rochester

Syracuse

Moline

The Jordan Era

In 1984, the Chicago Bulls got a blessing in the form of Michael Jordan. Jordan is not only the best basketball player of all time, but a marginally crappy baseball player, too. Jordan led the Bulls to six championships in eight years, and may have won more had he not donated the other two championships to charity. Jordan's game elevated the status of the NBA, attracting more mainstream fans and selling millions of sneakers.

Jordan was one of the first mass-marketed athletes, endorsing his own line of shoes, cologne, underwear, and gambling hotlines. Jordan's commercial appeal created a new market for NBA superstars like Vince Carter, Dwyane Wade, and LeBron James. Unfortunately, not all stars of Jordan's time were as marketable, as some looked like Patrick Ewing.

The National Basketball Association Goes International

1989 saw a rule change that allowed professional athletes to compete in Olympic play, since most countries had been cheating and doing it anyway. So in 1992, the United States assembled "The Dream Team," a basketball team built on a fantastic collection of future Hall of Famers and Christian Laettner. The team won their games by an average margin of 43.7 points. Coincidentally, that's the total points Christian Laettner scored last season. I'm kidding; Lattner's been out of the NBA for a while now.

The Dream Team was just the first step in the NBA's globalization of the 1990s. Just a little over a decade later, two of the best players in the NBA are Canadian (Steve Nash) and German (Dirk Nowitzki). Nash and Nowitzki are heroes in their native countries, having broken the NBA's new white color barrier.

Countries That Will Probably Never Have an NBA Player

Iraq

Liechtenstein

Trinidad and or Tobago

Vatican City

True Fake Stat: 3

Fans standing on each other's shoulders to equal one Manute Bol.

The Women Strike Back

In 1997, the NBA continued its path toward global domination with the inaugural season of the WNBA – a professional league for women. While there have been plenty of women's leagues in the past, the WNBA was the first to contain the letters "NBA" in its name, and that's got to count for something. Despite the NBA selling off teams and a few of them folding, the league is still running. The WNBA now has thirteen teams, and at least nine of them should still exist by the time of publication.

How the WNBA Can Be More Like the NBA

A man comes forward accusing Dawn Staley of mothering five children with him. A confused Staley is quoted as saying, "I think I'd remember if I was the mother."

Tamika Catchings chokes her coach and is banned from the WNBA. She complains of the double standard, saying that when guys choke their coaches, they're seen as assertive and signed by the Knicks.

Cynthia Miller is showing off her baton twirling skills at her spacious New Jersey estate. However, she accidentally lets one get away, and it whacks her chauffer on the head. The bruise takes 2-3 days to fade.

Sue Bird announces her marriage to former Baywatch bombshell Carmen Electra. Men everywhere drool at the thought of the honeymoon.

Sheryl Swoopes brawls with a fan, kicks her dog, and changes her name to "Ron."

Take That, Every Other League

Now that the NBA is clearly the premiere basketball league (and possibly sports league), they're expanding with more than just teams. In 2001, the NBA started the National Basketball Development League, now simply known as the D-League. The D-League serves as a farm system for the NBA, though the majority of basketball players did not grow up on farms. While most D-League clubs are shared by 2-3 NBA teams, the Lakers bought their own because they had $20. The D-League has now begun absorbing teams from the Continental Basketball Association, and we expect a merger with the WNBA shortly.

Is the Game Too Flashy?

With all the glitz now associated with the NBA, the game itself has suffered. Fundamentals are long gone, and the only traveling called is by a team's travel agents. The game has become about the fast break and the dunk, and quiet players like Tim Duncan are overlooked in favor of flashier personalities like Dennis Rodman, Allen Iverson, and Spike Lee.

Many purists lament that the college game is better than the NBA since it is more focused on the team. The pro game is focused on people who nickname themselves "Starbury." Ultra purists would want a basket that requires a poking stick, so hopefully they don't exist.

A League of Thugs?

While basketball is currently at its height of popularity and fans are captivated for several months of the NBA playoffs, the game has had a few black eyes. Not black guys, it has more than a few of them.

Anyway, the Portland Trail Blazers are often nicknamed the Jail Blazers because of all the thugs they employ. Players like Ron Artest, Allen Iverson, and Stephen Jackson seem to get more fouls off the court than on (see what I did there?). Even high profile players like Kobe Bryant are sometimes linked with scandal. Not the rape thing but the utter inability to shut his mouth thing.

Commissioner David Stern is working hard to clean up the league, partly by working on character-building programs and partly by excusing the behavior of players. Hopefully the new rule that players must play at least one year of college ball will help mature them a bit. Because if there's one group of people who get emotionally grounded, its star basketball players for college teams.

David Stern's Excuses for Ron Artest's Behavior

Cruelty to animals:
"He was feeding his dog plenty. The dog just wasn't eating."

Domestic battery:
"He was just trying to high-five her."

Brawling with fans:
"That was aired on television! There's no excuse for that!"

The Future

The NBA is aggressively marketing its young stars, until those stars get arrested or brawl during a game. Players like LeBron James and Dwyane Wade have become ambassadors of the game and all the product endorsement that comes with it. Wade and LeBron do so many commercials that the only products they don't endorse are each other. And that's only a matter of time.

"Hi, this is LeBron James, here to tell you about the new and improved Dwyane Wade. He can be yours, for just four easy payments of $3.1 million."

CHAPTER THREE

Football: The Longest GM Ad in History

Beginnings

What we call "soccer" in America, Europeans call "football." What we call "football" in America, Europeans call "that game Americans play." What we call "war" in America, Europeans call "Tuesday." Now that the terms are straight, let's begin.

The origin of American football is a long and confusing one, but we know a few things for sure. First, a rudimentary version was being played in Jamestown, Virginia in the early 17th century. Second, in the 1820s, reports of other versions of the game were being played at Harvard, Dartmouth, and the school that later became Princeton. That was the last time any team in the Ivy League won a football game.

Football in Europe at the time was divided into two types. One was the kicking game, which would later become soccer. Two was the running game, which would later become rugby. People in Massachusetts however, combined the two into some sort of hybrid. That version slowly gained popularity in the states, thanks in no small part to the charming smile of Tom Brady.

Rutgers v. Princeton

On November 6th, 1869, the first intercollegiate football game was played with a set of pretty retarded rules. Players couldn't run with the ball or throw the ball, there were no touchdowns, and it was played with a round ball. According to the Rutgers website, there were twenty-five members to a team, divided into eleven "fielders" and twelve "bulldogs." Twenty-five players divided into groups of eleven and twelve. The other two players must have been busy trying to count to twenty-five.

Somehow, most historians still count this as a football game.

Other Things Rutgers is Better At Than Princeton Aside From Football

Being located in New Bruinswick.

Starting with the letter "R."

Having fewer students in sweaters.

Is it Football Yet?

In 1873, Yale, Columbia, Princeton, and Rutgers got together and wrote down a bunch of rules that sound a lot like soccer. Harvard chose to skip the meeting, partially because their version involved running with the ball, and partially because they were busy thinking they were better than everyone.

Thankfully, Harvard's stubbornness actually helped change the game to a more rugby-esque version. A few years later, Harvard met with Yale, Columbia, and Princeton to determine a set of rules that involved running with the ball.

They meant to invite Rutgers, too, but dude, they totally spaced. Hey, sorry man, you can come to the next one, k? We still buds?

In the next decade, Yale coach Walter Camp finally developed a version of the game that seems at least recognizable, introducing elements like the offensive line, downs, scrimmage, and the Dallas Cowboys Cheerleaders.

The First Pro

Football didn't truly become a professional sport until 1920, because most people thought being paid to play ball was dishonorable. Keep in mind, this wasn't too long after the whole "earth was flat" debacle.

The first professional football player was William "Refrigerator Perry" Heffelfinger, who was paid $500 for one game in 1892. That may seem like nothing now, but back then $500 was enough to buy an entire run-down tenement building.

Other Things $500 Could Buy in the 19th Century

A house
A small farm
A horse
A slave

Necessary Roughness

Early football was so violent that in 1905, 18 players were killed. And Ray Lewis swears he didn't see anything.

In stepped Theodore Roosevelt, who asked for reforms to the game's basic structure. He also suggested that football's governing body should be called "Roosevelt's Rapscallions" and that they'd ride together through the countryside defending football's honor.

Innovations like the forward pass, the fourth down, and the neutral zone were developed. And though 33 people were still killed playing football in 1908, the game eventually became less violent. Now the only deaths are at gun point during the off-season.

True Fake Stat: 0

Football games played before padding where no one cried.

The Rise of the NFL

The first successful pro leagues were regional leagues, where most of the teams were funded by local companies. The most notable was the Ohio league, with teams like The Canton Bulldogs and the Massillon Tigers. Canton later became the locale for the Football Hall of Fame. Massillon has a Wal-Mart.

The American Professional Football Association began in 1920, with 14 teams mainly in the Midwest. Sort of like the World Series always taking place in North America. Many of the teams were in small towns, like Hammond, Decatur, and Muncie. Today, those three towns also have Wal-Marts. Green Bay was the only small town to keep its team to this day, making the Packers the longest lasting professional football franchise. Part of their success back then came from a young quarterback named Brett Favre.

In 1921, the league changed its name to the NFL, though it was not yet the powerhouse it is today. Teams came and went, including the Oorang Indians, an all-Native American team that also put on a dog show. Really. They were a football team that put on a dog show. I did the research for this book, and I still don't understand that one.

> **Should a Football Team Ever Also Put on a Dog Show?**
>
> No.

Early Stars

The success of the college game helped the early pro game, as college stars often broke out in the pros. Unlike Danny Wuerffel.

The first football star was Jim Thorpe, a gold meal Olympian named after a small town in Pennsylvania. Thorpe also played professional basketball and baseball. Take that Bo Jackson.

Other early pro stars included former college standouts Red Grange and Benny Friedman. Yes, the legendary Benny Friedman. Friedman, the first great passer, was finally enshrined in the Football Hall of Fame in 2005. Up 'til then, most people thought Benny Friedman was the NFL's first accountant.

The Early Early Genesis of the Super Bowl

In 1932, the Chicago Bears and Portsmouth Spartans tied for first place, prompting football fans everywhere to look up Portsmouth on a map. Turns out it's in Ohio. The tie also prompted a playoff game, which was so successful that the NFL divided into two divisions the following year to introduce a championship. It was a revolutionary idea, having already been utilized in baseball for the last three decades.

It would be another 34 years before the championship was called "The Super Bowl," but Pepsi was already spending a billion dollars on sub-par commercials.

Really? Owners Went to War?

In 1943, rich people still had a conscience, and so some owners joined players in the service. Both owners of the then Cleveland Rams enlisted, and the team was granted permission to take the year off. Which is what the Detroit Lions have been doing since the late nineties.

One of the oddest side effects of the war was the mergers between teams due to depleted rosters. First the Pittsburgh Steelers merged with the Philadelphia Eagles for a season to become Phil-Pitt. The following year, Pittsburgh merged with the Cardinals and were called Card-Pitt. The year after that, Boston and Brooklyn merged, too. Fans were thrilled when the war ended, partly because their boys came home safe and partly because they had no idea who was playing for what team. Kind of like free agency.

By the end of the war, 631 NFL players had served and 21 had died in action. That might sound like a lot until you remember that's way fewer than the number who were killed on field in 1908.

The Move West

Baseball was not the first sport to move west, as the Cleveland Rams became the Los Angeles Rams in 1946. The Rams also signed Kenny Washington and Woody Strode, the first black players of the modern era. It was the beginning of the end for football in Los Angeles.

Okay, so that's not why Los Angeles doesn't have a football team today. Los Angeles doesn't have a football team because no one in LA cares about sports unless it helps them land a client or a role.

> **Other Big Cities Aside From Los Angeles That Don't Have Football Teams**
>
> Hollywood
>
> Santa Monica
>
> East Los Angeles

The Requisite Rival League

In 1946, the All-America Football Conference tried to challenge the NFL for supremacy. As usually happens, the league was swallowed up a few years later, but not before producing the Cleveland Browns and San Francisco 49ers. Thankfully the NFL did not take the AAFC's New York Yankees or Brooklyn Dodgers because that would have been very confusing. Yes, all three of New York's football teams had the exact same names as their baseball teams. Real clever, guys.

The challenge of the AAFC was over and the NFL reigned supreme. Eventually. 1952 finally marked the last time an NFL team folded, when the brand new Dallas Texans gave up mid-season. If only the Houston Texans would consider doing that now.

After 1952, there were no more merged teams and folded franchises. The NFL was now beginning to take the shape we recognize today. You know, a big ol' commercial.

The NFL and TV

The NFL was the first major league to really embrace television, leading to its immense growth. In 1950, the Los Angeles Rams had all of their games televised. Bear in mind, that was before they sucked. In 1951, the Rams won the first nationally-televised championship game, defeating the Cleveland Browns. All seven people who could afford TVs tuned in.

The 1958 NFL championship game was an overtime thriller between Johnny Unitas's Colts and Kathy Lee Gifford's husband's New York Giants. The Colts were coached by Weeb Eubank, and I'm only mentioning that so I can use the word "Weeb." The game was a huge event for the NFL, as a record number of viewers tuned in to see the Giants blow the big one. That would be tradition for years to come. Not watching football on TV, but watching the Giants lose on TV. The Giants lost five championship games in six years.

The NFL reaching fans via TV would also become a tradition, thanks in no small part to NFL Films. While Major League Baseball was convinced that airing their games on TV would somehow hurt attendance, the NFL was made up of people who were not idiots. By 1964, the NFL bought out the small company that filmed their championship games and began producing highlight reels for each team. Which is impressive, considering how bad some teams are. I'd love to see the highlight film for the 0-14 1976 Tampa Bay Buccaneers.

"Well, no one died. Go Bucs!"

NFL Films is known for using orchestral scores to portray football games as epic battles. It's a surprisingly successful technique, considering many football fans think a visit to the Cracker Barrel is a cultural outing.

Monday Night Football was another key factor in the success of the NFL. In 1964, commissioner Pete Rozelle tried to have a Friday night game, which critics defeated due to the conflict with (get this) high school football. Those critics all lived in West Texas.

Rozelle instead scheduled a Monday night game and drew a record crowd. The league began televising a few Monday night games per season, finally signing a weekly contract with ABC in 1970. Monday Night Football has had its share of problems – mainly on air drinking, airing teams with poor records late in the season, and Dennis Miller. But overall, it is one of the most successful television ventures of all time, and helped the NFL dominate the sports landscape. Especially the Midwestern fat guy sports landscape.

Great Moments in NFL TV History

Howard Cosell Gets Drunk on Monday Night Football.
Don Meredith Gets Drunk on Monday Night Football.
Joe Namath Gets Drunk on Saturday Night Football.

A Second Rival League?

As the NFL began taking off, a new league called The American Football League sprang up. The two leagues began warring for players and blah blah blah, you know the deal. Same as any time this happens – the leagues eventually make nice and merge. But this time, one offshoot was created – a bowl game between the AFL and NFL champions. A bowl that would be so great in stature, we might even call it super.

Before the leagues merged, the two champions played each other in the first Super Bowl. Some think the NFL planned to use the game to show that the AFL couldn't hang and should take their ball and go home. And it looked like that at first.

The first two Super Bowls weren't very exciting, with the Green Bay Packers handily defeating whatever garbage the AFL threw at them. But Super Bowl III featured a dramatic upset – Joe Namath led the New York Jets to a surprise defeat of the Baltimore Colts. It would be the last game the Jets ever won. The MVP award was given to Namath's fur coat.

Once fans saw that the AFL could compete, the two leagues merged and the Super Bowl became tradition. There were now twenty six teams in the NFL, and at least four of them were good.

The Brief Dynasties

The tradition in football is to have a team that is virtually unbeatable for five years that then sucks for a lot longer. The Miami Dolphins played in three straight Super Bowls (1972-1974) and had to wait eight years before making another one. The Pittsburgh Steelers won four Super Bowls from 1975-1980, and didn't even get to lose another one until 1996. The

Oakland Raiders won two out of five (1977 and 1981) and had a twenty-one year layoff before they got another shot at it. So the point is if you don't win the big one during your dynasty, you may have to watch it for the next few decades. I'm looking at you, Buffalo.

The Draft

The NFL started their draft in 1936, with the Eagles making original Heisman winner Jay Berwanger the first overall pick, ever. Berwanger decided not to turn pro and ended up manufacturing plastic car parts. Good call, Jay. The third pick was made by the Pittsburgh Pirates (who later became the Steelers). They drafted a guy named William Shakespeare out of Notre Dame. Shakespeare also never turned pro, and ended up manufacturing plays.

Back then the draft consisted of nine rounds and no fans attended. It was probably better then, because now every pick gets booed. "Man, they took that guy I never heard of! I wanted them to take that guy I kinda heard of!"

The draft has changed much since that first year, especially in 1965 when the league instated the rule to only draft college graduates. The rule is a bit of a formality, as many football schools will graduate any football player who can pronounce his own name. But the league's heart was in the right place.

The rule has since been changed to force players to wait three years after high school for the draft. Maurice Clarett challenged that rule unsuccessfully, much in the way he challenged Ohio law enforcement.

More Ch-Ch-Ch Changes

In 1970, three major rule changes were instituted. First, the Point After Touchdown was made to be worth one point, because hey, that's what it's called. Second, the scoreboard clock was made the official timer of the game – though I'm not sure what it was there for otherwise. I guess just for show. Finally, surnames were added to the backs of jerseys. Thankfully that year, no one was named "He Hate Me."

In 1973, the NFL finally took steps towards eliminating their retarded blackout rule. Before 1973, the NFL wouldn't broadcast games locally in order to increase attendance. Okay, maybe some of the guys that ran football were idiots, too. When league officials realized that they could make way more money in merchandising and ad revenue than they could in ticket sales and hot dogs, the NFL let up and aired the Super Bowl where it was being played. Really, that used to be against the rules. At first, only games that were sold out at least three days before the game were aired in their local markets, and only thanks to a law passed by Congress. Odd when the most visionary entity in a story is the United States Congress.

Standard jersey numbers were also adopted. Quarterbacks and specialists were given 1-19, 20-49 was saved for running backs and defensive backs, 50-59 for centers and linebackers, 60-79 went to defensive linemen and interior offensive linemen other than centers, and 80-89 went to wide receivers and tight ends. Later on, 90-99 would be given to defensive linemen and linebackers as well. And A529720 would be reserved for inmate Maurice Clarett.

A Third Rival League? You've Got To Be Kidding Me

In 1974, a third rival league began play, this time called the World Football League because they were running out of names. The WFL was founded by Gary Davidson, the same guy who started the American Basketball Association and the World Hockey Association. Davidson was less of a businessman and sports fan and really just liked to cause trouble for people writing books about sports.

This time, however, he failed miserably. The league started successfully, signing more than 60 players away from the NFL including marquee names like Larry Csonka and Ken Stabler. Attendance was huge as well, averaging just under 43,000 for the first week. Too bad most of those tickets were giveaways – and by week six, some of the teams were already trying to relocate. In the second season, news came out that players were being fed by local families, and one team even had their uniforms impounded when they couldn't pay a cleaning bill. So they threw the World Series.

The league folded partway through the second season and no teams were invited to join the NFL. And Gary Davidson thankfully did not try to mess with Major League Baseball.

Sunday Is No Longer The Lord's Day

The NFL's relationship with TV continued, as they somehow negotiated a broadcast deal with all three major networks for broadcast rights. ABC got Monday Night Football, four prime time games, the Pro Bowl, and the Hall of Fame games. CBS got the NFC games that were left. NBC got the AFC games that were left and the next two Super Bowls. Fox did not exist yet, but they probably would have bid for the rights to cheerleaders.

Now football was all over television, even in local markets (freaking finally). Sundays became football day as the average American could flip between several games at a time. They wouldn't, because this was long before remote controls. But they could have. Churches took a serious hit in attendance, except when guys showed up to pray for their team that was playing Monday night.

True Fake Stat: 2

Football fans who also shop at Pottery Barn.

There's No Striking in Football! There's No Striking in Football!

Just in case football was getting too popular, the National Football League Players Association struck on September 20th, 1982. After seven weeks of hiatus, play resumed in November. No one told the Tampa Bay Buccaneers, who didn't start playing again until the late Nineties.

The strike was about the collective bargaining agreement, mainly league minimums. Under the new agreement, training camp and post-season pay were increased, a salary structure was established for veterans, retirement benefits increased, and all players named Joe were now nicknamed "Weeb."

The strike didn't damage the NFL much as ratings and attendance went up the next year. But it did make room for the United States Football League, a fourth competitor.

A Fourth Rival League? @$%#!!!!

Seriously guys, stop. Another freaking league? This time, the competing league wasn't really competing, playing its games in the spring instead. With big college names like Herschel Walker, Doug Flutie, Reggie White, and Jim Kelly, some thought that the USFL posed a serious threat to the NFL. Those people must not have read the rest of this chapter.

After three years of teams folding and relocating, the USFL decided to move their games to the fall and compete directly with the NFL. Good call, guys. But before that season, the USFL sued the NFL over an illegal monopoly and won-- kind of. The verdict was $1 in damages. The bad news is that the jury ruled that most of the problems the USFL faced were due to its own mismanagement. The good news is that under anti-trust law, verdicts are tripled, so the USFL really won $3.

USFL operations were suspended immediately, so Reggie White was free to sign with the Packers and be racist.

> **Other Names for Leagues That Could Eventually Compete With the NFL**
> North American Football League
> Football League of America
> National American Football League
> League of American Football
> Arena Football

San Francisco Learns to Pass

After leading Notre Dame to a national championship and being widely regarded as one of top quarterbacks in the college game, Joe Montana was inexplicably drafted 82nd overall by the San Francisco 49ers. He sat behind Steve DeBerg his first season before taking over during year two and never looking back, except to laugh at Steve DeBerg. Coincidentally, a quarterback named Jack Thompson was the third overall pick. Why coincidentally? He lasted three years in Cincinnati before landing in Tampa Bay and being benched in favor of Steve DeBerg. So there.

In 1981, Montana led the 49ers to their first Super Bowl win, a 26-21 victory over – wow – Jack Thompson and the Cincinnati Bengals. Montana led the 49ers to three more Super Bowls, and Thompson retired to sell insurance.

Montana was eventually injured in 1991, opening the door for Steve Young. Young was another Hall of Fame passer, leading the 49ers to another Super Bowl win in 1995. Young retired in 1999, and so did the 49ers.

The 49ers were fortunate enough to have two dynasties in a row. Now they're so bad they're not even allowed to watch the Super Bowl.

Drafts Problems of the 1990s

1990 – The New York Jets used their second overall pick to draft running back Blair Thomas, passing on Emmitt Smith.

1991 – Thin year – 10 picks before anyone selected a wide receiver, running back, or quarterback.

1992 – The Broncos drafted QB Tommy Maddox. Not only did they already have John Freaking Elway, but it was 10 years before Maddox would actually be any good.

1993 – Trent Green went 222nd overall. But the Seattle Seahawks taking Rick Mirer with their second overall pick was a solid move.

1994 – Finally, a strong draft. Eight of the top thirteen picks have made the Pro Bowl. Of course, the first overall pick did not.

1995 – Five running backs and three wide receivers went in the first round, including first overall pick Ki-Jana Carter. Not a single one has made a Pro Bowl.

1996 – Keyshawn Johnson, Terrell Owens, Lawrence Phillips, and Ray Lewis were all drafted. And none of them have gotten into trouble since.

1997 – One of the weakest drafts ever. When the best player in the first round is a tight end, that's a weak draft.

1998 – Ryan Leaf.

1999 – The Cleveland Browns drafted QB Tim Couch over both Donovan McNabb and Daunte Culpepper. How'd that turn out?

The NFL Around the World

The NFL played its first game in Mexico City in 1978, when the Saints and the Eagles scrimmaged before the season. There's no record as to whether or not the game was blacked out from the local broadcast.

In the 1980s, the NFL added preseason games in London. In 1990, that expanded to Tokyo, Berlin, and Montreal. That year, the NFL also founded the World League of American Football, which was thankfully not a competing league. It eventually morphed into the World League and eventually NFL Europe and then NFL Europa. Until folding in 2007, the league consisted of five teams in Germany and one in Amsterdam. Teams in England, Spain, and Scotland folded quickly – possibly due to many players' desire to play in Amsterdam instead. Curious.

NFL Europa served as the testing ground for many rule changes, including the two-point conversion and the shorter kick off tee. But the idea of audio coverage of single players and helmet cameras was nixed when it was discovered that football players tend to swear like football players

Disparity in the NFL Doesn't Matter

Only seventeen franchises have ever won a Super Bowl – that's barely more than half the 32 playing today. Heck, there are six teams that have never even made the Super Bowl. But the amazing thing about football is that fans can watch a game even if they care nothing about the teams. If that wasn't the case, Detroit Lions fans would shut off their TVs in December.

Is there competitive disparity in the NFL? Of course. Does it hurt the game? Not really. There's a fifteen-year waiting list for Jets and Giants season tickets. The only way to get tickets to a Packers game is to have them willed to you. And the Detroit Lions are consistently awful and they still average over 60,000 fans per game. That's over a quarter million fans per win.

A Fifth Competing League? Make it Stop!

In 2001, WWF Owner Vince McMahon formed the XFL, a spring league set to compete with the NFL. Players were encouraged to have on-camera romances with cheerleaders, wore bizarre nicknames on their jerseys, and were broadcast by Minnesota governor and former wrestler Jesse Ventura. In other words, it was less football and more wrestling. The league folded due to atrocious TV ratings – a game actually set the record for the lowest Nielsen share of any primetime broadcast. Worse than any episode of "According to Jim." Congratulations Vince – that's hard to do.

The league folded after one season, mainly because no one took it seriously. It's hard to when your most notable player has a jersey that says "He Hate Me." Ironically, the player's real last name was "Smart."

I'm Going to Disneyworld After I Cash My Check

Because the Super Bowl is consistently the highest rated program of the year, advertising space is at a premium. The Super Bowl has produced some legendary commercials, including campaigns like "I'm Going to Disneyworld," "Nothin But Net," and "I Am Not a Crook." The Super Bowl is also responsible for the fame of the Budweiser Frogs, Bud Bowl, and Mean Joe Greene.

Ever since Macintosh's 1984 spoof of 1984, Super Bowl commercials have become part of the event. I'd estimate that half the people who watch the game now care more about the commercials than the teams playing. Especially in 2001. I'm a Giants fan and that game was boring. The average Super Bowl commercial now costs $2.5 million dollars. So if just a few more of you buy this book, I'm totally there next year.

The biggest controversy came in 2004, when Janet Jackson's bare breast ruined the lives of every American child who saw it for a split second and later Googled it due to all the controversy. Because of the "nudity," the Super Bowl has been much tamer since, no longer accepting ads for things like erectile dysfunction medicine. No, the Super Bowl is just about family things, like beer and credit cards.

Products You Will Never See Advertised During a Superbowl

Stayfresh

Lane Bryant

Sex and the City

Carrots

Bureau of Alcohol, Tobacco, and Rae Carruth

In 1994, the NFL began instituting the most comprehensive drug program in professional sports, partially because they had the most comprehensive druggies in professional sports. Over the years the program has certainly been tested, especially when Nate Newton was caught transporting 386 pounds of marijuana in one year. The man was worth his weight in pot.

Other severe tests to the drug policy included Sebastian Janikowski slipping himself ruffies, Todd Marinovich being nicknamed Marijuanavich, Bill Romanowski admitting to using every steroid out there, and Darrell Russell being banned indefinitely for repeated drug abuse and possibly videotaping a GHB-induced rape. But enough about the Oakland Raiders. The biggest test came when Ricky Williams, who publicly retired in favor of smoking pot, unretired only to fail another drug test.

The NFL is not always tough on criminal behavior. Just a few months after former first-round draft pick Rae Carruth hired a hit-man to kill his pregnant girlfriend, other first rounder Ray Lewis was at a murder scene. At the very least, Lewis saw two people murdered and kept quiet about it. But that season, he was allowed to both win a Super Bowl and the NFL's Defendant of the Year. Sorry, I meant Defender of the Year. I always screw that up.

Lately, new commissioner Roger Goodell has been tougher on off-field behavior, suspending Pacman Jones a full season for being named Pacman. Jones was involved in a strip club incident where three people were shot and $81,000 of Jones' money was confiscated. Good thing football isn't violent anymore. Teddy Roosevelt is rolling over in his grave. On a horse.

True Fake Stat: 0

Suspensions that have never been appealed.

CHAPTER FOUR

Hockey: Yes, It's Still a Sport

Beginnings

Unlike baseball, basketball, and football, hockey is not an American sport. It only became an American sport recently, when 7,000 NHL teams moved down here from Canada.

Field hockey has been played in Europe for hundreds of years, but field hockey is almost as boring as Europe, so we'll start with the beginnings of ice hockey. In 1875, the modern game was founded by J.G. Creighton in Montreal, Canada. J.G. probably stood for Jean George or something French, but the point is he was the first guy to write down rules that are anything like what we play today.

It's embarrassing how the game really started. Allegedly, Canadian Pierre Lapin swung his curved walking stick at a frozen beaver bladder. And the game spread when the Canadian Prime Minister offered a tea pot as a prize to the best team. I wish I was making this crap up.

Finally in 1885, North America's first amateur hockey league was formed, based in Kingston, Ontario and consisting of four teams. Within a few years, hockey fan Lord Stanley of Preston bought a silver bowl with a gold interior and awarded it to the best team. It was thankfully a bit nicer than a teapot, and started the tradition of the Stanley Cup. The one awarded today is a bit bigger.

> **Rejected Ideas For Hockey Trophys**
>
> The Stanley Steamer
> The Stanley Kowalski
> The Flat Stanley
> The Stan Lee

Anything You Can Do, We Can Do Also

The game also caught on in America, and the first professional league was formed in 1904. Called the International Pro Hockey League, it was based in the Upper Peninsula of Michigan because there's nothing else to do there. Several other leagues were popping up and folding consisting of Canadian and American teams, until the Pacific Coast League and the National Hockey Association were stable enough to play each other for Lord Stanley's Cup.

A few more leagues were formed and disbanded, and the NHA pretty much evaporated once World War I hit. Though at the time, it wasn't called World War I because no one knew there'd be a second one.

Give it Back!

While America was busy fighting a war, Canada decided to keep playing hockey, forming the National Hockey League.

That's right – that N doesn't stand for America. The original NHL consisted of five teams in Canada. The NHL played the PCL for the Stanley Cup until the PCL folded in 1926.

The NHL did not start strong. Due to conflicts with a previous NHA owner, a fire that destroyed the Montreal arena, and a flu epidemic, the league was down to three teams at one point. But thanks to escalated salaries, no other Canadian league could afford to compete. The NHL expanded rapidly and contracted rapidly, until it was left with six teams in 1942: The Boston Bruins, Chicago Blackhawks, Detroit Redwings, Montreal Canadiens, New York Rangers, and Toronto Maple Leafs. These are known as the original six, even though the Canadiens are the only team that was actually part of the original NHL. Maybe "original" means something different in French.

Let's Go Rangers?

A six-team league is barely a league, but because there were no other competing leagues, the NHL still remained the dominant force in hockey. Oddly enough, the Norris family owned a piece of all four American teams. But for some reason people enjoyed it, and the league survived on six teams owned by three families for twenty five years. So the fact that the New York Rangers didn't win the Cup in all that time is even more pathetic. Winning the Cup back then was like winning the division now.

In the 25-year span of the original six, the Rangers only even made it to the finals once. In 25 years, the Rangers couldn't even finish second. As a Ranger fan myself, I'd like to show you the math on this.

There is roughly an 83% chance that one particular team will not win the Cup in any given season, so your favorite team will probably not win. The odds that any one of the six teams will not win the Cup two seasons in a row is 5/6 * 5/6 – or 69%. That number keeps dwindling exponentially the more years you add to the equation. So, all things equal in a six-team league, the odds that the Rangers would NOT win a Cup for 25 years are approximately 1%. Congratulations, boys – you completely defied the odds.

In fairness, the Boston Bruins didn't win a cup those 25 years either, but at least they had the chance to lose five of them. I'd tell you the odds of a team finishing second only once but my calculator would laugh at me.

Excuses for the Rangers Not Even Finishing Second In a League of Six

"Six may seem like only a few now, but you have to factor in inflation."

"We were too busy watching the Yankees."

"In a terrible coincidence, the whole team is allergic to MSG."

"Hey, Rangers are no good at baseball, either."

"Potvin sucks!"

Canada, Eh?

While it's hard to say that any team in a six-team league is a dynasty, the Toronto Maple Leafs and the Montreal Canadiens convinced me otherwise. The New York Rangers did not.

In the early Forties, The Maple Leafs won the Stanley Cup three times in three years, and two of them in a sweep. They won five Cups in seven seasons, including 1942, when they won despite dropping the first three games of the series to the Red Wings.

The next dynasty belonged to the Canadiens, who won the Stanley Cups five straight years from 1956-1960. The Canadiens also won four in a row from 1976-1979, a feat much more impressive considering there were more than six teams by then. The franchise has won the Cup twenty-four times, which is thirty-two more than the Los Angeles Kings.

The Maple Leafs regained supremacy in the early Sixties when they three-peated again. From 1956-1969, all but one Stanley Cup went to Montreal or Toronto. In 1961 the Cup went to the Chicago Blackhawks, and it's the last time they've seen it since. And, perhaps, ever.

The Original Six Are Boring

By 1967, the minor success of the minor Western Hockey League scared the NHL into adding the Philadelphia Flyers, St. Louis Blues, Minnesota North Stars, Los Angeles Kings, Oakland Seals, and Pittsburgh Penguins. Three years later, they also added the Vancouver Canucks and Buffalo Sabres. The only continuity in the league is that the Rangers still did not win a Stanley Cup.

The Oakland Seals were nothing more than an attempt to keep the WHL as a minor league. They were originally part of the WHL as the San Francisco Seals, but they were bought, moved, and absorbed by the NHL. The team folded after nine seasons. But the NHL fended off a challenger and was safe for another two years.

> **The Benefits of Having a Hockey Team in Oakland**
>
> Drive-by face-offs.
>
> Tons of ice, albeit not the kind you need to play hockey.
>
> High sticking seems tame in comparison.
>
> No one is distracted by a good football team.

Anybody's Ballgame

Because there were now way more expansion teams than original teams, it was easy for a new team to grab a championship. Or at least make it there. In their first three years of existence, the St. Louis Blues were swept in the Stanley Cup finals three times. Those are the only three times the Blues have seen the promised land, making them a solid 0-12 in Stanley Cup Games. Go Blues!

It wasn't long before expansion teams actually began winning, when the Philadelphia Flyers became the first non-original six team to win a Stanley Cup since the advent of the original six. The Flyers were nicknamed "The Broad Street Bullies," less because of league MVP Bobby Clarke and more because of Dave Schultz's hours and hours of penalty minutes. The Flyers won the Cup in 1974 and 1975 before the Canadiens finished the decade with another four Cup wins.

More Expansion, More Expansion!

In 1972, it was the World Hockey Association's turn to challenge the NHL, which caused the NHL to scramble and create the New York Islanders and the Atlanta Flames solely to block the WHA entries to new arenas. In 1974, the NHL also added the Kansas City Scouts and Washington Capitals. The Scouts had to move within two years, and quality of play around the league was horrifically diluted. But the important part is the NHL got another league to fold. In fact, the WHA did just that at the end of the 1978-79 season. The remaining four teams joined the NHL: The Edmonton Oilers, Hartford Whalers, Quebec Nordiques, and Winnipeg Jets.

For twenty-five years, the NHL had six teams. In twelve years following that period, they'd grown to more than three times that size. And it wasn't over. The NHL would face many challenges ahead trying to prevent a further diluting of the talent pool, generating interest in new markets, and preventing the Rangers from winning a Stanley Cup.

Who Wants Fishsticks?

From 1980-83, the New York Islanders won four straight Stanley Cups – a feat not really unprecedented since the Canadiens had just done it. But the important part was that these guys were new, playing in a major market, and dominating. It hurts every Ranger fan bone in my body to say it, but the early-Eighties Islanders were one of the best dynasties in sports history. They didn't just win the Stanley Cup Finals four straight years – they swept it twice. Their last vanquished opponent was the Edmonton Oilers, a team that was about to win the Cup five times in the next seven years. And they were playing in a field of twenty-one teams, not six. If you can count the Rangers as a team.

A Candid Conversation Between Two People From Long Island About the Islanders

"Hey, did you, like, see the game?"

"I did, I did. How about yourself?"

"Yah. Want to go to a diner?"

The Great One

It is surprising that by 1979, no player in any sport had ever been nicknamed "The Great One." Sure, a few people called themselves that but it never really stuck. In his rookie season, Wayne Gretzky won the first of his eight consecutive MVP awards, and, well, deserved that nickname.

Over the course of his career, Gretzky set forty regular season records, fifteen playoff records, and six all-star records. He also had a nice mullet. More importantly, he led his Edmonton Oilers to repeated Stanley Cups. Gretzky was so dominant that he doesn't just have more all-time points than the next guy – he has more goals OR assists than the next guy.

What's the Answer to Half Filled Arenas? More Expansion!

Despite the NHL's clear #4 ranking behind the NFL, NBA, and MLB, the 1990s saw even more expansion. The NHL added nine more teams in nine years, with the San Jose Sharks (1991), Ottawa Senators and Tampa Bay Lightning (1992), Mighty Ducks of Anaheim and Florida Panthers (1993), Nashville Predators (1998), Atlanta Thrashers (1999), and Minnesota Wild and Columbus Blue Jackets (2000). At least three of those teams can still sell tickets.

The NHL's overexpansion is one of the main reasons for the league's struggles today. Many teams are in warm weather climates where kids don't grow up playing hockey. In the meantime, many big, cold-weather cities are without teams: Seattle, Milwaukee, and Portland being the most obvious choices. Of course, if any league officials are reading this they'll probably expand there, too, so I'm sorry if that printed.

Let's Go Rangers!

In 1994, something historic happened: the Rangers stopped sucking and won a Stanley Cup. Rest assured, they've pretty much sucked since. But man, what a year.

Let's Go Home!

The Rangers were almost reigning champions in 1995, too, because a lockout threatened to cancel the season. The NHL's timing could not have been worse. With the baseball season just cancelled due to labor problems, the other three leagues were fighting for fans looking for a new favorite sport. The NBA and NFL should really thank the NHL for all the fans hockey didn't gain in 1994. At the very least, they should send a fruit basket.

The NHL's result was a new collective bargaining agreement, a shortened 48-game season, and a number of disillusioned fans. With baseball's strike clearly being about the money, it was not hard for hockey fans to assume their lockout was similar. The main issue to owners and players was a salary cap. The main issue to fans was the 468 cancelled games. Potato, potatoe.

> **What Hockey Fans Did To Occupy Their Time During the Lockout**
>
> Hit frozen beaver bladders across the ice.
>
> Followed the baseball strike.

Canada Declares Inherent Inferiority

In five years, four NHL franchises relocated, confusing everybody. In 1993, the Minnesota North Stars became the Dallas Stars. That one is easy to remember. In 1995, The Quebec Nordiques became the Colorado Avalanche. In 1996, the Winnipeg Jets became the Phoenix Coyotes. And in 1997, the Hartford Whalers became the Carolina Hurricanes. Those three are not as easy.

The moves were significant for three main reasons. First, all four teams moved from cold weather cities to warm weather cities. Except Hartford, all three areas that lost teams were hockey-crazed, and it took many by surprise that those markets could no longer support teams. Second, two Canadian teams moved to America, leaving just six north of the border. Six teams! That's barely enough to have a league for twenty-five years. And third, three of the four teams have already won Stanley Cups in their new cities. The new cities don't support hockey any more than the old cities – the teams just stopped sucking.

Detroit's Return to Prominence

In 1997, the Detroit Red Wings hadn't won a Stanley Cup since 1955. Now that the Rangers won theirs, the once proud Red Wings were in the longest draught in hockey. That changed quickly. Thanks to a collection of about 75 future Hall of Famers including a few unretired retirees, the Scotty Bowman-led Red Wings won two straight Stanley Cup Finals, and another one four years later.

The longest Stanley Cup draught now belongs to the Chicago Blackhawks and, like I said, will probably stay that way.

Parity is For Suckers

In the 1990s, the NHL was finally getting interesting. In the 21 years following the 1967 expansion, only five teams won the Stanley Cup. That's the least parity in the history of the four major leagues. But with the exception of Detroit bringing back the dead to win another championship, there have been no dynasties post-Edmonton.

In the 16 Stanley Cup Finals that have been played since 1990, ten teams have hoisted the Cup. So things are better, right? The NHL is thriving, right? More and more kids become hockey fans every day, right? In the words of many great authors before me: no.

We Didn't Want to Play Anyway

The labor agreement negotiated during the lockout expired in September 2004. So as any good commissioner would, Gary Bettman announced a lockout of the Players' Union and temporarily closed the NHL head office. Yippee. That's probably worse than ending the all-star game in a tie.

When the players finally returned to the ice 310 days later, the NHL had set the record for the longest shutdown in sports history. An entire season was cancelled, which could have spelled death for the league. But when the players returned, they returned to record attendance figures, including year-long sellouts for the Colorado Avalanche, the Montreal Canadiens, and the Vancouver Canucks. The increased attendance numbers are partially due to a lack of a decent TV contract. Seriously, what the hell is Versus?

The Versus network, which broadcasts the vast majority of regular season games aired in America, is not nearly the giant ESPN is. Heck, Versus isn't even the giant that ESPN Deportes is. While attendance is up, TV ratings have plummeted for hockey, dropping to barely over 50% of what they were. So, long-term, that lockout was a GREAT idea. Thank you, Mr. Bettman.

Guess Which Show Is Actually Aired on Versus

E-Force

Fusion TV

Holy @#%*!

IFSA Strongman

Lucas Oil Motorsport Hour

RacerTV

Shark Hunters: East vs. West

Team Spirit

PBR Built Ford Tough Series Presented By Wrangler

Louis Vuitton Cup

Giro D

Wanted Ted or Alive

Answer: They're all real, because that network is ridiculous. Louis Vuitton Cup? Wow.

CHAPTER FIVE

Soccer, Golf, and Other Sports That Don't Deserve Their Own Chapters

Bodybuilding

Beginnings

In the late 19th century, a Prussian man named Eugen Sandow created shows around displaying his toned physique. For some reason, people paid to see that, and a sport was born. Perhaps Sandow needed something to do, what with his country about to disappear.

The first bodybuilding contest was organized by Sandow in 1901, where the winner received a statue of Sandow. Really. One of the judges was also Sherlock Holmes creator Sir Arthur Conan Doyle. Because this story couldn't get any more bizarre.

The Golden Age

1940-1970 was known as the golden age of body building, with a shift towards muscle mass rather than symmetry and definition. The bodybuilding world will tell you the shift was due to more boys training for World War II and getting bigger and stronger. It had nothing to do with the coincidental invention of the anabolic steroid in the 1930s.

In this time, Mr. Universe and Mr. Olympia were both established. Today, Mr. Olympia is the most respected event in bodybuilding, and it's probably judged by J.K. Rowling.

I'll Be Back

Arnold Schwarzenegger's 1977 film "Pumping Iron" helped bring bodybuilding to the mainstream. Finally, everyday people could see how bizarre and freakish it was. In 1990, the WWF's Vince MacMahon opened his own competing body-building league, which folded within three years. It was not called the XBL.

Today, bodybuilding is campaigning for acceptance as an Olympic sport. Which will probably never happen, but no one thought Arnold Schwarzenegger would be governor of California, either.

Famous Bodybuilders

Eugen Sandow

Arnold Schwarzenegger

Popeye

Bowling

Beginnings

Any sport where the athletes are fatter than the fans is hardly a sport at all. But for any kid who grew up without cable, it's hard not to mention bowling. Bowling was all I had to watch on a Sunday afternoon, which makes me wonder how little there really was on TV in the late Eighties.

Bowling can be traced back as far as you want to trace it if you bothered looking it up. But good old American 10-pin bowling has its roots in organized crime. In 1841 Connecticut, nine-pin bowling was banned due to increased gambling and racketeering, so players added a tenth pin to get around the law. Which makes me wonder how little there really was to do in Connecticut in the 18th century.

The first indoor bowling alley was Knickerbockers in New York City, built in 1840. The alley was named for a crappy basketball team. In 1895, bowlers founded the American Bowling Congress, which is like the American Bowling Senate except they have more elected members.

The Virus Spreads

In 1920, there were 450 sanctioned bowling alleys in America. In 1929, that increased to 2,000. Now, there are that many just in suburban Pennsylvania.

The growth of bowling happened mainly in the 1940s and 1950s, when the world was a great big sock hop. Bowling alleys became great places to take your date before you dry humped in your car. Technology also helped spur on growth, with automatic pin setters replacing "pin boys," who would later become boxers.

In the sixties, America abandoned bowling for more fun things like war and sex. But technology helped again, introducing computer scoring so the average American no longer needed to understand the complex rules of the game. You know, all five of them.

Bowling was rejuvenated, and although a bowling alley is no longer the optimum date place, many fat middle-aged people now go there and act like they're athletes. In the lane next to a kid rolling the ball between his legs.

True Fake Stat: 8

Guys who have ever gotten laid due to their bowling prowess.

The Biggest Sport?

While professional bowling never truly caught on the way that, say, anything else did, semi-professional bowling is immensely popular. Bowling has more registered, dues-paying members than any other sport, and it is estimated that bowlers spend more on airlines, restaurants, and hotels than any other "athletes." In fairness, many bowlers are forced to buy two airplane tickets at a time.

Boxing

Beginnings

Fist-fighting has been around as long as man could say, "what's that about my mother?" But it didn't officially become a sport until the Olympics adopted it in 688 BC. That year, Theseus was defeated by a young George Foreman.

Actually, Theseus's version of the sport involved two men, sitting across from each other, punching each other until one died. So he was more of an ultimate fighter than a boxer. Early versions of boxing also involved two men standing, wearing spiked gloves and nothing else. The sport is a lot more watchable today.

In 18th-century England, a much more recognizable version of boxing became popular. Two British men would beat the hell out of each other with bare knuckles, and by the end of the fight their teeth would be in better shape than when they started.

Queensbury?

The boxing that we have come to know is governed by rules based on the Marquees of Queensbury. The Queensbury rules were published in 1867 as a way to prevent wrestling, give rests between rounds, and make someone named "Queensbury" seem cool. Bare knuckle fights were also outlawed, and fights started to actually become strategic. Most of all, the Queensbury Rules civilized the sport, outlawing most of the barbaric elements that ruled boxing, including Mike Tyson.

Who Boxes?

The best boxers traditionally come from the lower class, mainly because they grew up learning to fight. Also, rich parents actually care if their kids get the snot beaten out of them. Here's a look at the timeline of the lower class in America through boxing:

> Irish
> Italian
> Jewish
> Middle European
> Black
> Latino
> Arab
> Whoever we oppress next

Beginnings

Chess has been virtually the same since the late 15th century, when it was used to decide whose land Christopher Columbus would eventually claim as undiscovered. The oldest known chess guide was printed in 1497, back when people only had dot matrix printers.

In the 18th and 19th centuries, chess was a popular staple of coffee houses. Eventually, the open mic was invented and chess moved on. By 1843, a German chess master published the first comprehensive manual of chess theory. The Germans really could have used that guy a century later to tell them not to fight a two-front war.

Early Pawns

In 1851, England hosted the first international chess tournament. By 1886, the championship was standardized and has remained virtually the same since. Like paintball.

One thing chess features that most sports don't is the concept of a recurring champion. Emanuel Lasker held his world championship for 27 years. In contrast, poker players usually defend their world championships by losing to some kid who plays a lot online.

Current Kings

Russian people are better at chess than everyone else.

Cycling

Cycling has featured international competition since the turn of the century, and isn't quite as popular as it used to be since we now have cars. The Tour de France was first organized in 1903, but didn't feature whole-sale drug use until at least a few years later.

Diving

Most dives we see today were banned from the early sport. At the turn of the century, diving was a simple jump that was done head first. Oooh, fancy. Eventually, the sport added a bit of flair by adding a twist, a turn, a run, and divers picking their dives out of a hat. Thankfully, that last aspect of the sport is now gone. No one wants to see all those hats getting wet.

Today, diving is incredibly complex. This is partially due to technology of springboards, and partially due to the runaway popularity of the movie "Back to School."

Figure Skating

Beginnings

While printed accounts of skating competitions in England exist as early as 1772, the British competitions were much more rigid than the style we're used to. Hmmm – the British, rigid. Who'd have thunk it.

Anyway, the modern style was introduced by American skater Jackson Haines. His free style (not freestyle) gradually became the norm, and by 1896 the first World Championship was held. Women were quickly banned from competition. Because when a bunch of guys are in leotards on skates, adding a woman would be totally gay.

A separate competition was developed for women, and it eventually became entertaining. The men are still working on that.

People Start to Care

While Sonja Henie parlayed her skating success into an acting career, most skaters toiled in anonymity until television. TV put more emphasis on athleticism and power, and skaters started attempting bigger, more impressive jumps. By 1990, women were triple jumping and men were quadruple jumping. Figure skating became one of the biggest events in the Winter Olympics, partially because there are no big events in the Winter Olympics.

> **Figure Skating's Competition in the Winter Olympics**
>
> Curling
>
> Ice Dancing
>
> Snowboardcross
>
> Luge
>
> Biathalon
>
> Cross Country Skiing
>
> Making Snow Angels

Beginnings

The oldest recorded game of golf is 1456, long before you needed express written consent of the PGA to record a game. To put that in perspective, golf was around before Christopher Columbus was even old enough to sail around the world giving people syphilis.

The myth that golf stands for "Gentlemen Only, Ladies Forbidden" is, well, a myth. "Golf" probably derives from Scottish or Dutch terms for striking something – for instance, a gentleman striking a lady because she got in the way of his golf game.

Golf spread very quickly among the upper class, who were taking many more trips around the world than the lower class. By the turn of the 20th century, there were already dozens of amateur tournaments, the PGA was being established, and slavery was outlawed. That last part paved the way for Tiger Woods.

Professionalism

In 1901, the Professional Golfers' Association was established in Great Britain and Ireland. In 1916, the PGA of America was established so we wouldn't have to deal with those silly English. Though they did make good allies in World War I.

Even while PGA Tour events like the Los Angeles Open began popping up around America, golf remained a predominantly amateur game well into the 19th century. When Bobby Jones won the original Grand Slam, the money went to those that bet on him. Jones himself earned hardly anything – he'd have been better off with a Grand Slam at Denny's. Though everyone who plays golf is rich anyway, so who cares?

It wasn't until 1954 that there was a $100,000 purse, and it wasn't until 1988 that a golfer made $1 million in a season. Which is still probably less than the interest on his trust fund.

When People Stopped Hating It

Golf has always been an amateur centered game, with fewer people following golf and more people playing it to get a leg up in business or both legs out of the house. However, Tiger Woods electrified the golf world by becoming the first black guy to win anything. Well, he's part black, anyway. That counts, right?

Tiger's youth, smile, and skin color captured America's attention as he quickly became one of the (if not the) best golfers of all time. He is clearly the best golfer to ever be named "Tiger."

Gymnastics

Beginnings

Gymnastics may be the oldest sport if you don't count animal sacrifice. In ancient Greece, every city had a gymnasia – a courtyard designed for running, jumping, and dodgeball. But when early Christians believed that our bodies should not be altered, gymnastics went away for awhile. This is obviously before churches had gyms.

Gymnastics made a comeback, however, when the late 18th century saw a few physical educators (read: gym teachers) designing exercises to make children more fit. Friedrich Ludwig Jahn built modern models of the horizontal bar, the parallel bars, and the vaulting horse. Unlike gymnasts in ancient Greece, Jahn did not use a real horse.

They Included What?

Part of the modern Olympics from their inception in 1896, gymnastics varied a great deal from year to year. Events included things like synchronized team calisthenics and rope climbing, which must have been thrilling to watch.

By 1954, the Olympics featured more standard events, like synchronized team rope climbing. The scoring system was also standardized to the 0-10 scale, which is usually used as a 9-10 scale. Still, it's better than the retarded 0-6 scale used in figure skating.

Modern gymnastics now features events like the parallel bars, as well as the pommel horse, rings, vault, and ogling of 14-year-old underdeveloped girls in tight outfits.

True Fake Stat: 0
Successful female gymnasts with size D breasts.

True Fake Stat: 52,639
Successful male bowlers with size D breasts.

Gymnastics: Rejected Ideas For Events

Pommel Cow

Wall Exercises

Uneven Parallel Bars

Falling Asleep

Calculus

Obstetric Ultrasound Imaging

Rope Climbing

Beginnings

By the times humans could write on something more than a wall, horse racing was already part of the culture. I am guessing a few early cave drawings say "$10 quiniela, numbers 3 and 7." And $10 was a lot back then.

Horse racing spread less for sport and more as a way to gamble. English knights imported Arab horses after the Crusades, mainly from the people they crusaded. Arab stallions known for speed were bred with English mares known for their endurance to produce speedy horses with endurance. That's how that stuff works. Nobility would often bet on whose horse was faster, as well as whose serf would be the first to die of the plague.

Match betting gave way to larger races during the reign of Queen Anne (who did not have sex with any of the horses). Spectators would bet on the races, a tradition still occasionally followed today. By 1750, England already had a regulating organization to oversee horse races. Which is impressive considering it took every other sport 'til about yesterday to get their act together. But when there's money involved, people move quicker.

Coming to America

After the Civil War, America's rich former slave owners were looking for a new way to step on the lower class, so gambling at the track became pretty popular. But as the century turned and anti-gambling sentiment rose, horse racing all but disappeared. Then, America had an epiphany. Gambling is only bad if you lose money, so once the states were allowed to keep a portion of the betting, racing resumed.

Horse Racing: What the Hell is a Julep?

The three biggest races today make up the Triple Crown: the Kentucky Derby, the Preakness, and the Belmont. Really the Derby is about 10 times the size of the other two combined, but if your sport doesn't have a triple crown or a grand slam, it's hardly a sport. 11 horses have won the Triple Crown, but none since Affirmed in 1978. And like any championship, the horses that win end up having a LOT of sex.

NASCAR

Beginnings

As most people know, NASCAR started when bootleggers would speed across the country to evade police during prohibition. Yet another annoying thing prohibition is responsible for.

When America repealed prohibition in 1933, bootleggers needed a way to make money and drunken hicks needed entertainment. The two came together like peanut butter and jelly. NASCAR was founded in 1948 by William France Sr. Odd, since NASCAR supporters today would criticize anything named "France."

The cars used in NASCAR are known as "stock cars" because they began as unaltered vehicles, as opposed to cars specifically designed for racing. Today, the cars are modified for safety and performance, but the body of the car is still "stock," especially all the advertisements along the sides. That looks just like the cars you and I drive.

Sports' Bastard Child

It wasn't until 1980 that America was able to see a race from start to finish on television. Races started airing the previous year, but 1980 was the first time anyone in rural North Carolina got television reception.

Over the years, NASCAR has gained in popularity, going from a curiosity to part of our everyday sports landscape. And like all American sports, NASCAR has faced its share of hardship on the way up. For instance, NASCAR had a color barrier just like any other sport. And it seems to get broken just about every twenty years. That's right – there are at least three black guys to have competed in a NASCAR event. Take that, racism!

So, to recap, NASCAR is a sport founded by criminals, especially popular among low income families in the rural southeast, and still has an unspoken color barrier. But even without all that to add to the fun, watching cars do laps is really exciting.

I Was Kidding, NASCAR is Fun, Please Don't Fire Bomb My House

See subject line for details.

Paintball

In 1976, two friends in New Hampshire wanted to recreate The Most Dangerous Game. You know, that story where two hunters try to kill each other? Well one of them stumbled upon a paintball gun, previously used to mark cattle from a distance. The two designed a twelve-man game and a sport was born.

Actually, it only spread because one of the 12 was Bob Jones, a writer for *Sports Illustrated*. Jones chronicled the event and a sport was born.

Actually, it wasn't until the early 1980s that guns with more than ten rounds, water-soluble paints, and facemasks were introduced. And then, a sport was born.

Poker

While poker has been played in America since at least the 1840s, it didn't truly become popular as a sport until the last few years, when every college kid with a laptop became convinced he could become a professional poker player.

The World Series of Poker hit the airwaves just as online poker was hitting the internet, increasing the craze. It is hard to tell if poker will gain or lose in popularity in the future. However, it is easy to tell that a sport where some of the best players in the world are fat old guys is not quite a sport. No offense, baseball.

Basic Odds

Three of a Kind: **35-1**

Straight: **132-1**

Royal Flush: **649,740-1**

An online poker player smelling bad: **20:1**

An online poker player having a girlfriend: **20:1**

A rich online poker player having a girlfriend even though he smells bad: **1:1**

An online poker player being mad at me for writing this: **1:1**

An online poker player stopping play to do anything about it: **100:1**

Two Pair: **13-1**

Polo

Polo actually began as a military training program in 6th-century Persia. And nothing that comes from the military in Iran could possibly be bad. While the game was often played by anyone with a horse, it became tradition for military and royalty to participate. Not with the commoners, of course. That'd be silly. The first known set of rules came in 1874, when the British decided that they wanted to colonize polo.

Today, just about everyone plays polo. Why, there's hardly an inner city street without a 300 yards long by 160 yards wide polo field. And all you have to do to start practicing is own a horse, which costs only a bit more than owning and maintaining a car. Oh, and have seven friends who also have horses.

Sailing

Beginnings

The America's Cup is the oldest active international trophy, first awarded in 1851. The legend goes that the ship "America" beat its competitors around England's Isle of Wight by twenty minutes. Yes, sailing is such a white sport that even the first competition was held around the Isle of Wight. Queen Victoria allegedly asked who came in second, and someone allegedly replied "there is no second, your majesty." Hardy har har har har we hate poor people.

The trophy was donated to the New York Yacht Club soon after, and the club established a friendly international competition among the upper class. Does anyone else find it wrong that New York had a Yacht Club before it had a tenement law?

USA! USA!

The New York Yacht Club, and thus America, successfully defended the cup for the next 113 years. That's the longest winning streak in the history of sports; take that, Atlanta Braves. England was pretty pissed, too – they were supposed to be the naval power and here America was kicking their ascots. To this day, England has never won the cup – the Brits are 0-11. That's the longest losing streak in the history of sports. Take that, New York Rangers.

The race is not run every year, or even with any regularity. Sometimes races are held two years apart, sometimes twenty-one years apart. Jeez, England – even the Mets win every twenty years. In 1983, Australia finally took the cup from America. Other winners include New Zealand (twice) and Switzerland, who won in their only race. The winning crew was showered with celebratory chocolate, watches, and blonde chicks. That last part is probably true.

Skiing

While skiing first started as a way to traverse unfriendly icy terrain like Norway and Minnesota, modern skiing came about in the 19th century when the Norwegian Sondre Norheim improved the bindings on skis to make turning easier. Before Norheim, skiers had to signal. Bindings kept improving, and rich kids in Colorado kept wanting to see their girlfriends in hot tubs. So skiing spread.

In 1924, the Federation Internationale de Ski was founded in France, which is why it has a French name. Today it's based in Switzerland because no one likes the French. I'm kidding – *viva la resistance!*

While competitive skiing is very popular in the Olympics, recreational skiing is even more popular. Entire towns have been built at the base of mountains to help provide accommodations, meals, and $10 cups of coffee to the season's skiers. And who wouldn't want to hurl themselves down a mountain at speeds man was never meant to attain? Sane people, that's who. But there are only a few of them in the world, so skiing is quite popular.

> **Bad Thing to Say While Teaching Someone to Ski**
>
> "Ever hear of Claudine Longet?"

Soccer

Beginnings

A reminder: soccer is the game where no one but the goalie uses his hands. Football is the game where the Raiders suck.

While versions of soccer have been played since ancient times (like the Fifties), the game was in disarray until 1863. Before then, soccer was so varied that teams had to agree to rules before they played.

"Hey, no killing any of our players. House rules."

But in 1863, a number of British clubs met to form the Football Association and yell racist things at each other.

Kidding, that racist part wouldn't happen for another few years. Anyway, the Football Association was an amateur league, and professionalism was banned. Mainly because the FA didn't realize how much money they could make off of it. Soccer got its nickname from the word "Association" which was abbreviated to "soccer" because the English are a silly people.

In the early 1880s, professional teams started taking over. And so did England. Since England had colonies everywhere anyway, it wasn't too hard to influence them all to play soccer.

International Competition

Soccer is known as an international sport, with the fiercest rivalries coming during international play. While England was already playing Scotland in the 19th century, an international governing body was not founded until 1904, when seven European countries met in Paris to discuss their fondness for Jerry Lewis. FIFA was born, and so were many rivalries. The rivalries were furthered by a couple World Wars, which made it difficult to play a friendly game.

The World Cup first started in 1930, but due to most countries shooting at each other, it didn't really catch on until 1950. Played every four years, the World Cup is a constant reminder that Europe and South America are really good at soccer. In 1994, the United States actually made the tournament, which inspired many Americans to force their kids to start playing.

True Fake Stat: 0

Americans who don't play soccer, yet still understand it.

Hooliganism

Soccer is known for the intensity of its fans. And by intensity, I mean murderous rage. There have been so many soccer fan-related deaths that I can't possibly list them here. Especially since some soccer fans might get mad and kill me.

It is pretty commonplace to see violence at soccer games, with teams routinely having to play in empty stadiums due to the actions of their fans. Remember when a drunken fan attacked an umpire at a baseball game a few years ago? That's nothing compared to your average soccer season. Players have been killed for on-field mistakes, referees have been beaten for missed calls, and fans have been stampeded while running from other violence. But yeah, soccer is awesome. You should totally watch.

Speed Skating

It's like skating, but faster.

Strongman

I once saw a guy carry a rock in the shape of Africa really far.

Surfing

At the time of publication, Wikipedia reads that "Surfing was first recorded in Hawaii by lord peanut head of antartica." I am hoping that's not true.

There are two main types of surfers – those with commercial ties and those without. Those without are called "soul surfers" and often look down on the professional surfers who receive sponsorship or sell surf-related products. Sometimes soul surfers look up to them from the ground they are forced to sleep on.

One of the most well-known surfers of all-time was known as Bodhi, who looked kind of like Patrick Swayze and paid for his surfer lifestyle by robbing banks. And that's about as true as lord peanut head.

Surfing: How to Be a Soul Surfer

1) Refuse endorsements.

2) Quit your job.

3) Loudly criticize those who accept endorsements or have jobs.

4) Have rich parents that can support your habit.

Swimming

Beginnings

We've had swimming ever since man crawled out of the ocean and onto dry land. Unless you're a Creationist, in which case we've had swimming ever since God gave it to us, the non-evolved humans that we are.

Swimming was part of the first modern Olympics, but there's evidence of it being taken seriously much earlier than that. In 1538, a German professor of languages wrote a book about swimming. I'm not sure why a language professor would write about swimming, but maybe he lived near a big lake.

It's Not Just For Survival Anymore

In 1908, the first organization to govern swimming was formed. The rules mandated that every swimmer be in water and be swimming. It's a pretty simple sport. Competitive swimming now isn't much different from how it was then. Though in 1952, the breaststroke and the butterfly were accepted as two different styles. That was a big day.

Tennis

Beginnings

Tennis is not a new sport, as it can be traced back to ancient Greece. In the middle ages, "The Second Shepards' Play" featured a tennis ball as one of the gifts given to baby Jesus. Ahh, gold, frankincense, and Wilson.

The modern game, however, can be traced to the late 19th century, when Major Clopton Wingfield played a version as a way to get back at his parents for naming him "Clopton." Wingfield even patented his version of the game, which was retarded since the sport was a thousand years old at the time. He was unable to enforce his patent, but does still hold a patent on the name "Clopton." Seriously, Clopton?

Stay Home, Poor People

Tennis was another sport that spread rapidly among the rich, who needed something to occupy the time they didn't use up by working. In 1881, The United States National Lawn Tennis Association was formed to govern the rules and prevent any poor people from playing. As if they could afford racquets. Besides, they were too busy boxing.

Within a few years, tennis featured all four Grand Slam events and the Davis Cup, but it wasn't until 1968 that anyone made a living from tennis. That's right – tennis was mainly amateur until the late Sixties, mainly because tennis players didn't need the money. That's the true sign of an upper crust sport – one where athletes actually play for the love of the game. Crazy.

Women are Better?

Women began playing tennis around the same time as men, with the first national championship for women held just six years after the men's. Why did women gravitate towards tennis? One, it was a rich person's game, and rich men preferred their wives to play tennis rather than bang the help. Two, you can play tennis and still be hot. For some reason female golfers have to look like men, but female tennis players are usually pretty attractive. Could be the skirts.

To this day, women's tennis is still more popular than men's. In fact, women don't even have to be good at tennis to be famous. Like Anna Kournikova, who was probably one of the top thousand or so female tennis players in the world. But you could totally see her butt in that skirt.

Why Women's Tennis Is More Interesting Than Men's Tennis

Grace

Finesse

Poise

Elegance

Style

Hot Chicks

Beginnings

Track was the first sport; when the first Olympics were held in 776 BC, the only event was the foot race. Oooh, what an exciting Olympics. A foot race. Can I get tickets? There were other games soon after the Olympic Games, like the Pythian Games, the Nemean Games, the Isthmian Games, and the Board Games. Track & Field events were staples of all of them, mainly because running is pretty affordable.

Running From Stuff

Track remained a large part of military training throughout history, mainly because it helps to have troops that aren't fat guys. Several military schools claim to be the first to formalize rules and regulations of track & field, but I can't tell you which ones since I don't care.

In 1912, an international governing body was founded and named the IAFF which probably stands for something. Track & Field had already been part of the modern Olympics since 1896, so the governing body was a bit late. Still, they helped make important decisions like letting stuff continue the way it had been going for centuries.

Today

Yeah, things are still pretty much the same. Maybe the outfits are different.

Beginnings

Like basketball, volleyball was designed in Massachusetts in the late 19th century to be a less violent indoor sport. They really must have been beating the hell out of each other back then. Anyway, a YMCA phys ed director named William G. Morgan invented mintonette, which was his gay name for volleyball. The game was renamed volleyball within a year because of all the volleying. I have no idea what mintonette means.

Volleyball evolved quickly. By 1900, a new ball was designed for the sport. By 1916, the set and the spike were regular features. And by 1920, there was a limit to how many times one side could hit the ball. And how many times someone could say "mintonette" without getting his ass kicked.

It Took Fifty Years For Anyone To Like It

The first organized volleyball entity came in 1947. Before that, volleyball anarchy ravaged the countryside. But the Federation Internationale de Volleyball, which was for some reason French, started regulating the sport. Within a few years there were World Championships, and within a few more volleyball was featured in the Olympics.

Beach volleyball, a version of volleyball played in a forest, also caught on. FIVB started regulating beach volleyball in 1986, and got it into the Olympics ten years later. It's still not called mintonette.

CHAPTER SIX

College Sports: The Paid Athletes of Tomorrow Getting Paid Today

Beginnings

Inter-collegiate athletics began in America in 1852 when rowing clubs from Yale and Harvard met up in a contest of who had the nicest sweater. Intercollegiate games became more popular throughout the end of the century, especially as schools figured out what the hell to call football.

The NCAA didn't always regulate college sports. Before 1906, no one did. Sure, colleges played each other in many sports, but it wasn't until 1906 that it became regulated and profitable.

As a reminder, Theodore Roosevelt called for a conference to investigate why so many football players were dying and why Ray Lewis was keeping quiet. In 1906, that committee led to the Intercollegiate Athletic Association of the United States. Four years later, that became the NCAA. Eleven years later, the first championship was held and the subsequent revenue potential was obvious. Also, the NCAA truly cares about the well being of its student athletes. But mainly the revenue thing.

The NCAA Tournament

Known as March Madness, The Big Dance, and The Los Angeles Angels of Anaheim, the NCAA Tournament is a single elimination tournament featuring 64 of the most competent basketball teams in the country, 32 of which actually stand a chance. First founded in 1939, the NCAA Tournament used to be second tier compared to the NIT. But the NCAA wielded its power justly and threatened to ban any team that took a bid from the NIT. They're such nice people, really looking out for the students' best interests. But mainly the revenue thing.

The tourney started with eight teams and steadily grew until it reached 64 in 1985. The tournament has remained at 64 teams ever since because no one counts the play-in game.

Seeding for the NCAA tourney is done with all the precision of an epileptic playing operation, and the later rounds of the tournament usually consist of a bunch of "underdogs" who were really just seeded poorly. But that makes for exciting bracket play.

Speaking of brackets, the point of the tournament is to gamble. There are few offices in America without a March Madness pool, and most large sports media outlets offer prizes of millions of dollars. Is it odd that the NCAA, an organization that bans gambling, is responsible for more wagering than the Maloof Brothers? I'm sure they're just looking out for the students' best interests. Not that revenue thing.

How To Pick a Perfect Tournament Bracket

1) Always pick a 1 to beat a 16. That upset has never happened.

2) Consider home region advantage. College fans are intense.

3) How well is the women's team doing? The football team? Interest in sports at the school can motivate a team.

4) Buy a sports almanac from the future. When you go back in time, make sure that Biff Tannen never gets a hold of it.

College Football's Missing Playoff Game

Division I football is the only known sports entity without a playoff system. Hell, rock-paper-scissors has a championship tournament. By the way, my rock beats your paper. Eat it.

Prior to 1998, National Champions were selected by a vote. That's right, a vote. Thrilling. Now, they're selected by a vote and one game. Less boring, sure. But that's like saying that the Clippers are less corporate than the Lakers.

Even though it would be easy to just shorten the season and create a few weeks of playoffs, the consensus is that there's no playoff system because of the money that would be lost. In a playoff system, the winning schools would get a much larger share of the revenue generated by their games. So instead of devising a revenue split, we're forced to watch the GalleryFurniture.com Bowl.

BCS: Because Computers Suck

The current system to pick college football's national champion involves the BCS, an intricate computerized point system devised by the world's most intelligent monkeys. It has failed miserably almost every year. And yet, we still use it.

In 1999, Kansas State finished third and was passed over for eight bowl spots. In 2001, three teams could have legitimately laid claim to the number two spot. In 2002, Oregon was picked by every person living outside of Lincoln as the number two team but Nebraska got to play for the championship anyway. In 2003, USC and LSU played in different bowl games and tied for the championship. In 2005, three undefeated teams were left out of the final game. And 2007 is too complicated to even discuss.

But yeah, it's a great system. Way better than a playoff.

Other College Sports

The College World Series exists, sure, but most good baseball players don't even go to college. In the 1980s, the only two decent World Series' Most Oustanding Players were Terry Francona and Calvin Schiraldi. Others included Lee Plemel, Mike Senne, and Greg Elenna. A veritable Who's Who of people currently selling insurance. A good indicator of how small-time the College World Series is in 2004, Cal-State Fullerton won. Most people reading this do not know where Fullerton is.

For the most part, nobody cares about other college sports except those playing them. Iowa State continually dominates the NCAA wrestling world and you can't name any of their wrestlers. The NCAA Hockey Tournament routinely features teams from states that start with the letter M. And the only thing exciting to come out of college lacrosse is the Duke rape scandal.

Former Duke Standouts That Are Now Stars in the NBA

Shane Battier

Carlos Boozer

Elton Brand

Luol Deng

~~Chris Duhon~~

~~Mike Dunleavy~~

~~Daniel Ewing~~

~~Grant Hill~~

~~Bobby Hurley~~

~~Dahntay Jones~~

~~Christian Laettner~~

~~Corey Magette~~

~~Shavlik Randolph~~

~~JJ Reddick~~

~~Shelden Williams~~

College Basketball Dynasties

When most people think college basketball dynasties, they think Duke. Yes, Duke is truly the best team to constantly lose early in the tournament. But other schools actually win the thing.

UCLA men's basketball is possibly the greatest dynasty of any professional sport. I'm sorry, did I say professional? Yes, college basketball is strictly amateur. My mistake. UCLA won the tournament ten times in twelve years. Consider that no other school has won it ten times total. And all you Montreal Canadiens fans, keep your mouths shut. UCLA was playing against more than five other teams.

Other schools that are perennial contenders include UNC, Kentucky, Kansas, Ohio State, Louisville, Indiana, and even Duke. (See? I said something nice about them.) Since most high school athletes want to be seen on a national stage, a winning team can keep winning by recruiting through victory. So, yeah, good luck St. Johns.

College Football Dynasties

The first 32 national championships were split between Harvard, Yale, Princeton, and Penn, all Ivy League teams. Columbia couldn't even win back then. As college football started spreading, public schools became more dominant. The last time an Ivy League team won a national championship was Yale in 1927. Mainly because rich white kids aren't so good at football.

Notre Dame is an odd dynasty in that they've won 13 national championships, and most were spread out by several years. USC recently lost their chance to three-peat, but are still tied for the second most titles with Alabama. Other schools of note include Oklahoma, Michigan, Ohio State, Miami, Nebraska, and Minnesota before they started sucking.

Title IX

Title IX (pronounced "title icks") was a pretty big deal because it made schools give out scholarships in equal amounts to men's and women's sports. The common complaint is that football teams are so big that there are now fewer scholarships available for non-football playing men. Not really – no big sports school is scaling back their men's scholarships because of title nine – they're just throwing money at women, too. Great job, NCAA – now you're training men to throw money at women.

The First VIII Titles

Title I: Men's tennis must receive an equal amount of funding to men's tennis.

Title II: If you use the bridge while playing pool, you're a bitch.

Title III: Only one good college baseball player per season.

Title IV: All white basketball players must wear John Stockton size mini shorts.

Title V: Everyone shall assume their college football team will win it all every year.

Title VI: There's no crying in baseball.

Title VII: No accepting money from people the press knows about.

Title VIII: The Grapes of Wrath.

The Rich Get Richest

Top colleges coaches, aside from using their celebrity for book deals and speaking engagements, are often paid millions. Top college programs earn millions from ticket sales, licensing, and television. And top college athletes earn the right to compete for millions later in life. And we wonder why so many leave early for the pros.

Nick Saban signed an eight-year, $32 million dollar deal with the University of Alabama. He'll have probably left to coach somewhere else by the time you read this, but the point is he's making a LOT of money to coach an amateur team. Alabama University President Robert Witt makes exactly one tenth of that. In fairness, no one who works for Witt can shoot.

Bull Isn't Just For South Florida and Buffalo

The NCAA was originally founded to protect the lives of student athletes, but it allegedly looks out for their best interests, too. Well, not entirely. NCAA athletes are not allowed to get paid beyond their full scholarships. Which amount to about $120,000 at most schools, but that's pocket change compared to what they really make. Hookups and housing are currency to college students like cigarettes are to inmates. So even if student athletes weren't allowed to miss class and reap hidden benefits, they're still making bank.

Should student athletes get paid? Not necessarily. But they should also be provided with the skills they need to get a job above Wal-Mart greeter. Many Division I programs have terrible graduation rates, and the overall NCAA graduation rate is below the nation's average. Which is unfortunate considering many of these students spend much more time in the gym than in class. Way to prepare the kids for the real world. The show "The Real World," because that's the only other place they can get that free of a ride.

NCAA athletes are basically paid despite their amateur status, but not in comparison to the money they make for the school. Yeah, college sports are definitely all about a student's best interests.

Rules Violations

In 1952, the NCAA established a mechanism to punish rules violations. This mechanism, known to some as RoboGlobalEnforcer2000, punishes schools for their "lack of institutional control." It's a great system – a school feels behind so they cheat. Then the NCAA takes away their ability to recruit, so they fall further behind. And that doesn't make them want to cheat more.

Schools found guilty of impropriety are placed on probation, which doesn't really mean much. Currently, Ohio State is on probation and they made the championship game in basketball and football. They ought to be careful though, because if they're found in violation again they could be placed on double secret probation.

Sometimes the NCAA punishes an individual player by making them briefly ineligible. These punishments are usually for accepting gifts from boosters, using their celebrity to get perks, or actually attending classes.

Minor NCAA Infractions

Turning left without signaling.

Rocking a mullet.

Eating a piece of food that has been on the floor for more than five seconds.

Taking shotgun without calling it.

Good Programs

There are good college programs out there where the athletes actually get an education and excel at their chosen sport. Like, um, the one with, well, crap, I know there are a few out there. I totally saw a special on it once.

CHAPTER SEVEN

Fame: Someone Tell Shaquille O'Neal To Stop Rapping

Are Professional Athletes Better People?

Are professional athletes really better people? No. In fact, the vast majority of them cheat on their wives. Except WBNA players, who don't have wives because it's illegal to do that in America. But they would if they could. I'm sorry, I just insinuated that WNBA players are, gasp, professional athletes. I hope my editor catches that.

Athletes are more disciplined, yes. They're in better shape, and their lives are typically more entertaining. But that doesn't mean they're better. Cooler, yes. But not better.

There are nice people and jerks in every profession, but some fans think that every athlete will be a nice person. Not true. So when your favorite player was a jerk in college and is suddenly a jerk in the pros, don't be so surprised. Especially if he went to Nebraska.

Why Are Athletes Famous?

Unlike reality TV stars, heiresses, and reality TV stars that are heiresses, athletes deserve their fame. They worked their whole lives to get where they are, and once there they are entitled to a little indulgence. Especially because we base much of our days around them. Imagine if tens of thousands of people came to your job to watch you work. You'd have a bit of a big head, too. Not a Barry Bonds big head, but you get the idea.

Athletes are famous because people live and die with their skill. Soccer fans die for it while the rest of us live for it, but it's common to see real adults with real jobs and real families walking around in baseball hats like they're twelve. Their day is brighter when their team wins. Sorry, Detroit Lions fans. The sun will come out tomorrow. Or in a few years.

How To Behave Around Athletes

Like any celebrity, athletes are just normal people that the world simultaneously idolizes and hates. And they probably don't appreciate you yelling "you suck!" while they're on their way to dinner. They may suck at their chosen sport. But they're still a whole lot better at it than you.

Even if they weren't vastly better at sports than we are, professional athletes are forced not to care about their fans. And who forced them? We did. We're the same people who yell "you're a bum!" when a .350 hitter strikes out, and "trade him!" when a QB throws a few interceptions the week after a 4th quarter comeback. So when we do cheer, that doesn't destroy the wall we've already forced them to build.

But why do we act like this? The strangest part is that we do it because we want a piece of the fame. Fans bring banners less to say something and more to get on TV. If a fan just wanted to show their loyalty, they wouldn't do it with an acrostic for ESPN. Fans stand and yell and cheer and boo. And that's less because fans mean any of it and more because they want their section to notice them. And I can actually sympathize.

In 1999, the Mets were down by one to the rival Braves in the 14th inning of a playoff game. I was at the game, freezing under a Mets blanket I'd bought that day to keep warm. Rather than freeze my baseballs off in despair, I began running around the stands with my blanket as a cape. The Mets slowly rallied and Robin Ventura won the game with the now famous grand slam single. From Flushing to Times Square, other fans were hugging and high-fiving me. Partially because I kept my blanket cape on the whole time. I really felt like part of that victory, and I still tell the story. Sometimes I even tell it in print.

What would happen if one of us were given part of that fame – a day to taste of what the players deal with? What if one of us were put in for one play. And what if we botched it and someone booed us? We'd brush them off as a fan who doesn't know anything. And when we were in the stands the next day, we'd keep right on a-booin'.

If you do happen upon a professional athlete, do not give your opinion on their play. Good, bad, it doesn't matter – because we don't matter. The only thing a professional athlete would like to hear from a perfect stranger is "thank you." Tell them that you enjoy watching them play, and thank them for it. You'd be surprised at how appreciative they'll be. Unless they're Terrell Owens.

> **Bad Things To Say to Athletes While Trying to Get an Autograph**
>
> "You were great in Chicago. Now, not so much."
>
> "Ever sign a guy's ass?"
>
> "It's for my son. His name is 'To Whom It May Concern.'"
>
> "Mind if I get a lock of your hair with that?"
>
> "Can you sign this picture of you cheating on your wife?"

What Are Athletes Allowed to Do With Their Fame?

Athletes are allowed to do whatever ludicrous stuff they want to do with their fame, as long as it doesn't take away from them being athletes. Because that will take away from their fame, which will take away from their ability to do ludicrous stuff.

Many athletes have used their on-field prowess to do good things, like start charity organizations. Others have used their fame for evil, like going into politics. Still others end up going into entertainment-related fields, like theatre, music, or politics.

For some unknown reason, football lends well to acting, as more than ten of the twenty-five football players I profiled in chapter nine ended up in movies or on TV. A good football career can lead to a role in movies, TV, or a double homicide.

I encourage any aspiring professional athletes looking for a side career to pick one that suits them. Like any celebrity, a side career has to fit. Paris Hilton can easily become a model or an actress or a stripper. But when she tries to sing, that's an insult to those who can. It's a similar issue with basketball players. You can not be a rapper just because you like rap. That's sort of like a basketball fan thinking he has a jump shot because he watches *NBA Inside Stuff.*

True Fake Stat: 482

Basketball players that have also released a rap album.

To Rap or to Ball

Congratulations! You've become a successful basketball player in the NBA! You've spent your whole life learning how to block, box out, cross-over, defend, drive, dunk, dribble, fake, foul, guard, jump, lay up, pass, pivot, post, rebound, run, screen, shoot, slam, transition, and date white women. So what now? Should you continue to concentrate on your game? Of course not!

No, your best option is to release a rap album. Sure, you've got as much experience rapping as most rappers have playing basketball. But why should that stop you? Just because you don't have much talent or experience rapping doesn't mean you can't make a career of it. Just look at Shaquille O'Neal. Okay, that's a bad example. Maybe Ron Artest? No, that's a bad one too. Allen Iverson? Crap.

Okay, so there's never been an NBA player with a successful rap career. But why should that stop you? After all, plenty of stars have used their fame to cross over to music. Like Paris

Hilton. Or Lindsay Lohan. And Eddie Murphy. Damn. I'm sure there's a good example somewhere.

The first step is to announce your rap album long before you've ever recorded anything. Hype is key. You certainly know your talent won't help it sell, so creating a market demand years before a product exists is a great jumping-off point. Especially since the album will be so bad, a bridge will become your next jumping-off point.

Once you announce you're going to start rapping, hang out with rappers. Yes, they'll probably be pissed that they spent their whole lives working towards a goal that you feel you can accomplish with little to no effort. But that doesn't matter – you're richer than they are, and thus they'll hang out with you anyway. If you play for the Lakers or the Clippers, you live in Hollywood and are thus used to this kind of behavior.

Eventually you will have to record an album. Your best bet is to have a buddy who has never set foot in a studio before produce it. That will make the album really street. Or perhaps really suck. I get my "S" words confused.

Make sure that while you're recording it, you degrade a large group of people. Like women or white people or anyone with an ear for good music. That last one will be easy, since you have no talent as a rapper. Oh, and if you could get homosexuals in there, too, it'd mean a great deal of press.

So now you have inner hype and outer hype and a finished product. I'm sure you landed a deal from one of the various record labels that puts out whatever garbage they think will sell (read: all of them). So your distribution is coming along, too. A number of people will buy your album out of sheer curiosity, and then use it as a coaster. Some might even save it for ten years until it becomes sarcastic nostalgia.

"Hey, remember that terrible album by that basketball player? I still have a copy. Isn't that funny?"

The bad news is that you will not sell nearly enough albums to earn out your advance. The good news is that the negative hailstorm of publicity you receive from your offensive lyrics is enough to curb jersey sales, destroy locker room chemistry, and cause fans to boo you constantly. Why is that good news? Because you were on a losing team anyway – otherwise you wouldn't have had a long enough off-season to record and promote a rap album.

So now you get traded to a contender, full of great players that haven't been playing as great as they should because they're too busy promoting their rap albums. You help them reach the playoffs, where you get knocked out in the first round because you and your teammates are busy composing lyrics to your next offensive "songs."

Which is great, because you'll have that whole off-season to record a new album.

> **Are Athletes Allowed to Use Their Fame to Kill People and Get Away With It?**
>
> Not usually. Especially not rookies.

CHAPTER EIGHT

Fan is Short for Fanatic, Which is Short For Fanatical Nutcase

Beginnings

Early sports fans filled the Colosseum in Rome to see their favorite gladiators eaten by lions. Today, we watch soccer. So not much has changed.

The word "fan" might be short for "fanatic" – there's no definitive root of origin. Some speculate it's short for "fancy," a 19th-century British term for those that watch boxing. Still others think it's short for "fan out," which is what a group of sports fans does after cops disperse their riot.

However fans got their name, they are the reason sports exists. They're especially the reason sports pay so well. The athlete has a love-hate relationship with fans, as their life would be a lot easier without fans, but a lot less expensive, too.

Sports Radio

A great outlet of sports fans is sports radio. Sports radio ranges from wonderful to awful, depending less on the host and more on the caller. We've all heard a call like this:

> "I say the Mavericks should trade for Kobe. They could give up a couple of late draft picks and boom, unstoppable."

> "Why would the Lakers trade Kobe Bryant for a couple of late draft picks?"

> "Cuz the Mavericks rule, man!"

Replace the teams and player, and most of us have heard that call every Tuesday. If you do call sports radio, please do so when you have an intelligent point that HAS NOT BEEN MADE YET. If the previous caller beat you to it, hang up. No one is listening to hear you say, "yeah, what he said."

Also, make sure to speak in sound byte. Do not ramble – you had several minutes to think about what you wanted to say while you were on hold. Don't tell the host your history of being a fan before you ask him what he thinks of the current team. Okay, so you have been following a long time. Have you followed long enough to know how not to be boring on the radio?

And most of all, please do not tell us how you'd have handled the situation last night. We know exactly how you'd have handled it – on the couch in your living room because that's the closest you'll ever get to having the opportunity.

Reasons to Call Sports Radio

You have something new and interesting to say.

You dialed the wrong number.

True Fake Stat: **52**

Minutes out of every hour that a sports talk caller is calling just to say they've been on the radio.

The Differences Between Sports Fans

There are very few true sports fans, as most fans follow one or two sports over the others. Some sports specifically don't mix; very few hockey fans will be excited by NASCAR highlights. Except Carolina Hurricane fans.

While fan behavior has certain commonalities, each sport has its quirks. Baseball fans are more likely to collect cards, while soccer fans are more likely to beat each other senseless with a waffle maker. Each sport has its quirks.

Major League Baseball Fans

Baseball is my favorite sport but let's face it: baseball is boring. It is hard to go to a regular season game and be riveted by every play. Especially since most of our teams suck. Baseball fans, however, are quite resourceful, doing what they can to make a Diamondbacks/Pirates game tolerable.

Baseball fans creatively stave off that boredom, mainly by playing drinking games and chanting. Baseball fans love chanting – even if it doesn't make sense. I once saw Reggie Jackson peek out of the Shea Stadium press box. My section started chanting "Reggie! Reggie!" The rest of the stadium tried to join in, but not knowing what was happening, it quickly turned into a chorus of "Eddie! Eddie!" Let's go Mets.

Baseball fans also think they'll be playing that day. While most sports see fans show up in jerseys, baseball fans even bring gloves. Sure, that glove is for the foul balls. In the upper deck.

> **Baseball Sign Suggestions**
>
> **Anaheim Angels:**
> "I threw my rally monkey on the field the other day. Can I please have it back?"
>
> **Washington Nationals:**
> "Where can we move to next?"
>
> **Florida Marlins:**
> "Do we have to keep showing up?"
>
> **New York Yankees:**
> "We look forward to buying your wild card."
>
> **Oakland A's:**
> "Playoff loss, here we come!"
>
> **Minnesota Twins:**
> "Good things come in small markets."
>
> **Milwaukee Brewers:**
> "Our owner was the commissioner and all we got was this lousy franchise."

NBA Fans

NBA fans are into fast-paced, high-flying action. Or at least the five of them that can afford to go to the game. So many basketball tickets are taken up by corporations that the best available seats are usually in the parking lot.

Most NBA watching is done on TV, so fans usually show up in a shirt and tie, not in mesh shorts with their own ball. But they do think they can shoot, no matter how old, fat, and white they get. Leave a basketball on a court and watch what happens if a business man walks by. He will not only try to shoot, he'll dribble for a second as if he's being guarded, turn, fade, and miss the hoop by a solid foot. Then he'll blame it on a college injury.

Do not be fooled – not all basketball fans think retro jerseys are cool. Those supposed fans are actually rappers disguised as fans.

College Basketball Fans

Most college basketball fans aren't college basketball fans at all, as it's next to impossible to keep up with how quickly teams change. Most college basketball fans watch college basketball in March and pretend like they saw more than a few highlights the rest of the year.

Those that are fans of college basketball are usually fans of one particular team and don't follow the rest. In fairness, there are hundreds of teams. Even more if you count St. Johns.

Fans of a program usually have a connection to the school, like having graduated from there or wished they did while attending a nearby community college. The biggest programs draw fans because they play on campuses filled with students and because there's nothing else to do in most college towns. My apologies to the thriving metropolis of Urbana, Illinois.

Between graduation, transferring, the draft, and the local authorities, players are constantly leaving teams. So those that follow college basketball are obsessed. They won't follow other college teams, but they will follow every high school prospect in the country. Mainly because they want to know who will wear their favorite team's uniform on their way to declaring early for the draft.

WNBA Fans

I went to one WNBA game. If I heard "You Go Girl!" one more time, I'd have shot myself in the face.

NFL Fans

I have to give it to football fans – they're the most intense of American fans. Football fans will go to games in sub-zero weather to watch a losing team lose to a slightly less losing team. As I wrote earlier, to get Packer tickets, someone in your family has to die. And if Brett Favre is any indication, people in Green Bay don't age.

NFL fans are also intense while watching on TV. For NFL fans, Sundays become almost holy, as if the day was set aside for some sort of group religious observance. NFL fans also tend to be fatter than other sports fans, since it's quite fashionable to gorge yourself while watching a game. Also because football is popular in the Midwest.

College Football Fans

College football fans are usually NFL fans bored on Saturdays. College football has a higher retention rate of players than college basketball, but because roster sizes are so large, it's harder for an unknown team to beat a powerhouse. While there are more than 100 division I-A teams, there are really only a handful that anyone needs to keep track of.

There's no playoff system in college football, which allows college football fans to blab on ad nauseum about how their team is the best in the country despite not making a bowl game sponsored by a company we've heard of. If college football ever got off their fat ass and instituted a playoff system, many fans would actually hate it because they'd have to shut up and wait 'til next year.

College football is especially big in the South, partially because of the lack of anything else to do. My apologies to the thriving metropolis of Tuscaloosa, Alabama.

Things to Do in Tuscaloosa, Alabama

Go to a Crimson Tide Football Game.
Go to a Crimson Tide Basketball Game.
Go to a Waffle House.
Shoot Yourself in the Face.

Hockey Fans

Hockey fans are sports' black sheep. Usually a baseball fan also likes football, or a football fan also likes basketball. But if you like hockey, it's not because you like sports. It's because you like hockey. Or because you're Canadian.

Hockey fans love their sport so much, they kept it going when there were only six teams. Which is still absurd. Anyway, most cheers at hockey games are actually private jokes. At Ranger games, you'll hear "Let's Go Rangers!" But you'll also hear "Potvin sucks!" a cheer about a player who retired before many of the current fans were born.

Hockey also doesn't translate well to television, as the excitement and the action does not always surround the puck. Which is fine, because it's really hard to find hockey on TV anymore. This keeps arenas filled, because hockey fans need their fix. And they're certainly not subscribing to Versus to get it.

Soccer Fans

Soccer fans are typically Europeans who love soccer, South Americans who love soccer, or Americans who play soccer. Soccer fans are notoriously intense, as they're one of the few groups of fans willing to kill for their team (Raider fans aside).

Soccer fans usually follow the game so closely they take off of work for big games, which is probably why America is still a superpower despite our mismanagement. We don't grind to a halt every time someone yells, "Goooooooooooooooooooooal!"

Many soccer fans follow every league, no matter how big or small. It's rare that a baseball fan can tell you how the local semi-pro team is doing. But ask a soccer fan, and they'll break out a jersey and start singing.

True Fake Stat: 7

Soccer fans that have never seen a dead body.

NASCAR Fans

If hockey began moving south sooner, maybe we wouldn't have these people. But NASCAR fans are supportive, I'll give them that. They're so supportive, they'll often put their favorite driver's memorabilia all over their trailer. And before you get offended, relax. I'm just making fun of single-wide trailers. You double-wide people are fine.

Golf Fans

The few, the proud, the old men from Florida. Even with Tiger Woods, not many kids grow up playing golf, so not many kids grow up watching golf. The one sport that makes baseball interesting, golf is usually watched by those too old to find the remote control.

Tennis Fans

The most polite people in the sports world, tennis fans will actually stay quiet during a match. And if any get rowdy, they'll respect a good shushing. Try that at a Red Sox game and those fans will tell you exactly what they think of your mother. Tennis fans, on the other hand, are typically pretty civil. Except that guy who stabbed Monica Seles. He was a dick.

Different Types of Fans

Fans don't just differ between sports – there are also different types and levels of fans. Like casual, medium, and maniac who ruined his marriage.

Fans v. Crazy Fans

Sometimes fans take their fandom to the extreme. Here's a guide to acceptable fan behavior.

Fan: Paints his face in team colors.
Crazy Fan: Paints his house in team colors.

Fan: Gets section to start a wave.
Crazy Fan: Gets megaphone to start a wave.

Fan: Buys season tickets.
Crazy Fan: Buys season ticket.

Fan: Knows his favorite player's batting average.
Crazy Fan: Knows his favorite player's social security number.

Fan: Waits for an autograph at the players' parking lot.
Crazy Fan: Waits for an autograph at the player's house.

Fan: Collects baseball cards.
Crazy Fan: Collects baseball players.

Fan: Owns a jersey with his favorite player's name on it.
Crazy Fan: Owns a jersey with his favorite player's DNA on it.

Fan: Brings a banner to cheer on his team.
Crazy Fan: Brings a banner to clean up the blood stains.

The Casual Fan

The casual fan likes sports, but doesn't follow much anymore. Every now and then they'll catch some highlights, but they usually get all their sports news from their friends. That doesn't stop them from talking sports to fit in. They usually repeat what they heard on the radio that day, allowing you to make up stats to "prove" them wrong.

"What do you mean the Brewers will collapse before the end of the season? Milwaukee's best month is July! The last five years, they've got a .700 winning percentage after July 4th!"

If you don't get why that's funny, you're probably a casual fan.

The Medium Fan

The medium fan doesn't revolve their life completely around sports, but they revolve their mood around it. While still being able to maintain a job, wife, and kids, the sports fan will feel empty if they don't catch SportsCenter at least once a day. Usually twice.

The medium fan will make sure to catch big games, but doesn't need to follow every single play. Though a box score in the morning won't hurt. The sports fan will also attend games pretty regularly, and convince their casual fan friends to go in on season tickets, since they probably will get too busy to use theirs.

The Maniac Who Ruined His Marriage

The maniac will follow sports at the expense of their friends and family. Which they stopped having years ago. The maniac will even take a job that lets them see games, like, say, selling hot dogs at the ballpark. Or unemployment.

The Super Fan

A form of the maniac, the super fan wants to be a part of their team so much that they become a part of the stadium experience. Like the Jets Fireman – someone who follows their team so loudly and consistently that a game isn't the same without them. And while I appreciate the super fans of my teams, I wonder what a super fan's life is like outside the game. I'd imagine that under that fire helmet, there is a lonely man just wanting a hug. So feel free to volunteer because I'm not going near that freak.

Failed Superfans

The New York Jets Jet Pack Guy

The Seattle Mariners Flamboyantly Gay Sailor

The Duke Blueballed Devil

The Golden State Warrior Guy Who Stabs Himself

The San Diego Padres Cursing Priest

The Similarities Between Sports Fans

There are some characteristics that unite sports fans. And while we don't all do these constantly, I'd bet everyone reading this book has done each of these things at least once.

Second Guessing

There are two types of second guessing. The first is done by inserting oneself into a decision making scenario, like a critical substitution that went awry. Which is odd because no fan ever says, "I'd have substituted in that situation, but he didn't. And I'm glad he didn't because we won. I'd have totally screwed that up."

The other second guess is way more egregious, and is based on the misguided idea that any sports fan can be an athlete. "How could he take that pitch! I'd have swung there!" Sure – in the off chance that the Cubs called you in from your job in ink & toner sales, and you could even hold the bat against 90-mile-an-hour pitching without wetting yourself, you'd have had the uncanny natural ability to know the pitch would break into the strike zone. And if you happened to get the bat off your fatty shoulders, I'm sure it would have done a lot of good.

Of course, the second guesser can tell us their second guesses by calling into sports radio.

Saying "We"

You're not an athlete. You don't have a shoe deal, and you don't bang supermodels. And you're also not 6'6 and 220 lbs. So stop saying "we." Unless you're saying, "WE watched the game last night, and THEY won."

Getting Frustrated at Obvious Things

Sports fans ought to know the game they're following. So when a pitcher works a 0-2 count and then wastes a pitch, don't boo. That's part of the game. So your favorite player fouled a guy in a crucial situation – that's because he meant to. It's not the ref's fault for seeing it.

Booing Your Own Players

Unless someone did something beyond unreasonable (like, say, willingly played for the Royals), there's no reason to boo them. So someone's in a slump. The quickest way out of it is never to hear 20,000 people booing in unison. The quickest way out of it is to be traded away from the Mets.

True Fake Stat: 1
Number of times booing a player ever helped.

Blaming a Player for Not Signing

No one is obligated to sign a ball for your wiener kid. Especially when the kid doesn't even care about the ball and it's clearly daddy who wants the autograph. But many fans will fault players for not making the time to sign everything thrown in their face.

Every player should make some time for their fans. But their schedules and moods do not revolve around yours. The players who don't ever sign are jerks. But the player who doesn't sign because he's late for batting practice or had a bad day or doesn't like daddy shoving a ball in his face for his "kid's" collection is just a player. Leave him the hell alone.

Proper Ways to Ask For An Autograph

"Mr. LAST NAME, could you please sign my ball?"

"I'm so happy you're on TEAM NAME. Would you mind signing this ball?"

"(Click) Sign this ball or the kid gets it."

Unwavering Belief

Only one team can win the championship – so why do we all think our team will? Why do we not realize that there are rebuilding years, or in some cases, decades? There are

Royals fans right now saying "wait 'til next year!" For what, free Royals tickets?

Each year, 5-10 teams have a legitimate shot at the title. The rest do not. Hell, even when the NHL was only 6 teams, the Rangers were dead at the start of the season. Does that mean you should stop rooting for your teams? No – I was a Mets fan in the early Nineties. But it does mean that you should root for more reasonable goals. Like, say, a .500 winning percentage.

The Worst Possible Sports Upsets

Tiger Woods goes a year without winning a major. Or a tournament. Or an endorsement deal.

Dale Earnhardt Jr. finishes second in the standings, followed closely by Jeff Gordon and Kevin Harvick. In first? A soccer mom from Akron.

Anna Kournikova wins anything.

USC loses their season opener after getting shutout by Notre Dame. In basketball.

Brazil fails to qualify for the World Cup after a devastating loss to Uzbekistan.

I Am a Better Fan Than You

(a guest essay by the biggest fan there is)

Just so you know, you're not a real sports fan. I am a much better fan than you.

I don't just watch games on TV. I go to games. You may have your little game night with your friends, but I'm there. Yell at the TV all you want, I'm the guy yelling ON the TV. They can't hear you from your couch. Sure, they may not be able to hear me from the bleachers either, but at least I have a shot. And yeah, I sit in the bleachers. You can't start a wave from a private box. Real fans don't spend money on good seats. They spend it on merch.

You know how you wear a jersey to the game? I wear a different jersey to every home game. It's not enough to support the superstar. You've got to support the entire team. Sure, there are more home games than team members. But to be a true fan, you need to support the memory of who used to be on the team.

I also wear a different jersey to every road game. Because I travel with the team. That's right – you have a direct TV package that lets you see road games. Well I see road games with my own eyes. Which have team-colored contacts. I have more frequent flyer miles than you have miles on your car. You know – your car with a pathetic team flag hanging off the back window? You're not a true fan 'til you reupholster the front seat in ticket stubs.

You think your face painting is impressive? Mine's a tattoo. You might get all dolled up for a game but I'm a fan the whole season. And the off-season, too. Hell, my tattoos are so intricate that I look like I'm wearing the road and home jersey, depending on where you're standing.

And I always stand. I don't need a wussy stadium seat cushion because a true fan doesn't sit down on his team. A true fan stands up – and not just in crucial situations. Because when my team is out there, it is always a crucial situation. I don't care if it is a rebuilding year – they need to know I'm there for them.

I do, however, sit in stadium seats at home. I'm not just a fan when it's convenient. I'm a fan 24-7. I eat in stadium seats. I sleep in stadium seats. When I sleep. I've got to be alert in case they ever make a trade. I've got to be the first one blogging about it or I'm not a true fan.

You post to a message board. I RUN a message board. Seven, actually. Because my job as a fan isn't just to support the team – it's to support other fans. The more I support them, the more they can support the team. So the more I support the team.

And I don't just support my team – I un-support other teams. I call opposing players in the middle of the night and threaten to show their wives pictures of them in compromising positions. I don't even have the pictures. But if my boys needed me to take some, I would. I'm that big of a fan.

My wife and my kids never get in the way of me watching a game. You know why? Because I don't have any. They'd just be baggage, preventing me from cheering for the good guys. That's why I don't have a job either. Jobs are dead weight when you've got to support your boys. I had a job selling pretzels for the team for a while but I quit because I couldn't see the whole game. If you miss even thirty seconds of a game, you're not a true fan. Speaking of which, I've got to go. The game starts in seven hours and I have to prepare.

What? You're still here reading? And you call yourself a fan.

CHAPTER NINE

Ruthian Players, Like Babe Ruth

This chapter features some of the greatest players of all time. I'm sure I left out a few of your favorites, but they're only paying me so much to write this book. So really, come off it. (Years of play are in parenthesis, much like this sentence.)

Baseball

Hank Aaron (1954-1976)

Hank Aaron burst on the scene by hitting his 716th homerun twenty years after his rookie season. The Rookie of the Year and a 21-time All-Star, Aaron finally got recognition from mainstream America by breaking Babe Ruth's record for career home runs, retiring, and waiting 'til we weren't quite as racist. Which will happen any day now.

Yogi Berra (1946-1965)

Dropping out of school in the 8th grade, Yogi Berra is one of the most wildly quoted baseball players of all time. Yogi was known for his brilliant "Yogiisms" like "It's like déjà vu all over again;" "When you come to a fork in the road, take it;" and "We have nothing to fear but fear itself." Berra also was a three-time MVP and led teams in both leagues to the World Series, but that's not nearly as quotable.

Yogiisms Yogi Never Said

"When you come to a fork in the road, pick it up and wash it off."

"It gets late at the appropriate time out there."

"It ain't over 'til Rosie O'Donnell sings."

Barry Bonds (1986-Whenever his head explodes)

Without steroids, Barry Bonds would have been one of the greatest baseball players of all time. Now he's just a big cheating cheater-head. If Barry Bonds's life ever gets made into a movie, Michael Clarke Duncan should play the current Bonds, and Dave Chappelle should play Bonds when he was in Pittsburgh.

True Fake Stat: 1,784

Angry letters I will get from Barry Bonds and his giant melon head.

Roger Clemens (1984-2003, 2004, 2005, 2006, 2007)

Roger Clemens holds many records, including most Cy Young Awards (7), children whose name starts with K (4), and times retired (3). Clemens is one of the most dominant pitchers of all time, and the steroid allegations are completely unproven, or they may be true depending on what happens by the time this book is published.

Roberto Clemente (1955-1972)

The only baseball player with exactly 3,000 hits, Roberto Clemente was tragically killed in a plane crash on his way to deliver aid to Nicaraguan earthquake victims. Ever since, most famous people just send a check.

Ty Cobb (1905-1928)

What a prick.

Joe DiMaggio (1936-1951)

Joe DiMaggio's second greatest accomplishment was a 56-game hitting streak that still stands today. His greatest accomplishment was nailing Marilyn Monroe. An outfielder for the Yankees, DiMaggio led his team to nine World Championships in 13 years, and was known to frequent Dinky Donuts before he passed.

Lou Gehrig (1923-1939)

Lou Gehrig was perhaps the best first baseman to ever play the game, just ahead of fellow Columbia alum Gene Larkin. Nicknamed the Iron Horse for his ability to not succumb to a fatal illness, Lou Gehrig eventually succumbed to a fatal illness. Gehrig and Eddie Collins make Columbia the only college with two baseball Hall of Famers, partially because many Hall of Famers didn't even go to high school.

> **How Columbia Honors the Memory of Lou Gehrig**
>
> By sucking at sports, so he'll always be the school's greatest athlete.

Hank Greenberg (1930-1947)

Nicknamed "Hammerin' Hank" and "Jew Boy," some speculate Hank Greenberg would have been even better had he not constantly been concerned with money and controlling the media. Like many Jews, Greenberg was born in New York and died in Beverly Hills. Unlike many Jews, he was really freaking good at baseball.

Other Great Jewish Athletes

Sandy Koufax

Mark Spitz

Moses

Rickey Henderson (1979-2003)

The career leader in stolen bases, Rickey Henderson played well into his 80s, and for a record 47 different Major League Baseball teams. Widely considered baseball's best leadoff hitter, Rickey does what Rickey says Rickey does when Rickey is talking about Rickey. And Rickey Henderson talks in the third person so often, this paragraph could have been written by him.

Reggie Jackson (1967-1987)

Nicknamed Mr. October due to his appearance in the "Studs with Funny Haircuts" calendar, Jackson was also one of the most prolific post-season hitters of all time. Jackson helped the A's and the Yankees to multiple World Championships, and the Angels to several playoff losses. Jackson also struck out more times than anyone in history, except me in high school.

Walter Johnson (1907-1927)

Walter "Big Train" Johnson was one of the first sidearm pitchers not to suck. Actually, he was one of the greatest pitchers of all time, racking up a strike out record that would stand for 55 years until it was broken by Nolan Ryan, Steve Carlton, Gaylord Perry, Tom Seaver, Don Sutton, Bert Blyleven, Roger Clemens, and Randy Johnson. But before those eight guys, Johnson was the best.

Sandy Koufax (1955-1966)

Dodger ace Sandy Koufax famously skipped a game in the fall because it was Yom Kippur. As opposed to the current Dodgers who rarely play past June. Koufax had the four best consecutive years any pitcher has ever had before retiring at age 30. Unlike Roger Clemens who retired at age 41, 43, and 44.

Greg Maddux (1986-2011)

One of the weeniest looking pitchers ever, Greg Maddux dominated the 1990s, winning more games that decade than any other pitcher (or the New York Mets). At the time of this book's publication, Maddux is in his 782nd season in the majors.

True Fake Stat: 3

Professional athletes that look weenier than Greg Maddux.

Mickey Mantle (1951-1968)

Known to fans as "The Mick," Mantle was thankfully not Irish or that would be offensive. One of the biggest Yankee icons, Mantle was known for his carousing with women and frequent drinking. Alcohol eventually killed Mantle, who was probably relieved that he didn't die of women.

Willie Mays (1951-1973)

A fantastic centerfielder for the New York Giants, Willie Mays was one of the first black baseball players white people publicly rooted for. Mays was the original five tool player, able to hit, hit with power, run, throw, and dice thousands of julienne fries. Mays is remembered for "The Catch, a play where he ran down a long fly, caught it backwards, spun around to prevent the runner from tagging up, and saved a baby from a burning building.

Rejected Nicknames For Willie Mays

The Say Hey Young Adult

Johnny Goodcatch

That darker fellow

Stan Musial (1941-1963)

Stan "The Man" Musial won four National League MVP awards for the Cardinals and is one of the few professional athletes to be known as a classy guy. Seriously, the guy was nice to people. No motive, nothing. It's weird.

Cal Ripken Jr. (1981-2001)

The original power-hitting shortstop, Cal Ripken Jr. cemented his place in baseball history when he broke Lou Gehrig's record for consecutive games played. Gehirg would have played a few more had he not been dying during the streak. But yeah, Ripken's accomplishments are decent, too.

Jackie Robinson (1947-1956)

I can't write about baseball without mentioning Jackie Robinson. Or the NAACP will sue me. Robinson, known for being the first black major league baseball player, was also a decent second baseman. He was known for his ability to steal home, mainly because sports writers of the time enjoyed using the words "black" and "stealing" in the same sentence.

Pete Rose (1963-1986)

Pete Rose is the lifetime hits leader and one of the biggest hustlers to ever play the game. A manager could always gamble on Rose to come up big, as he was always a safe bet. Rose helped the Reds stake claim to a number of World Series, and he remains one of the greatest hitters to ever wage war on opposing pitching. You could put money on it.

Babe Ruth (1914-1935)

Named for a candy bar, Babe Ruth grew up in an orphanage where he ate many of the other children. Ruth is known by most as the best baseball player to ever not take steroids, setting hundreds of records that have all since been broken by big cheating cheater-heads. Except the all-time home run record, which was broken by Hank Aaron.

Nolan Ryan (1966-1993)

Playing in a record-tying 27 seasons, Nolan Ryan was one of the most overpowering pitchers the game has ever seen. His 5,714 strikeouts are 1,200 more than anyone else in history. Even more impressive is that not all of them were Reggie Jackson.

Tom Seaver (1967-1986)

It is fitting that Tom Seaver follows Nolan Ryan, as Seaver was one reason that Nolan Ryan only spent a few seasons with the New York Mets. A Seaver-led rotation brought the Mets their first World Series – so of course they traded him a few years later, too. Seaver routinely led the league in ERA, strikeouts, and wins, and holds the record for highest percentage of Hall of Fame votes. So yeah, good call Mets.

Ted Williams (1939-1960)

Boston's Ted Williams was nicknamed the "Splendid Splinter," which is ridiculous because lots of decent nicknames were available back then. Arguably the best pure hitter to ever play the game, Williams is currently cryogenically frozen and that's really creepy.

Cy Young (1890-1911)

Cy Young is both the winningest and losingest pitcher of all time, having pitched in every game in Boston Red Sox history. Young was the first baseball player to have an award named after him, followed soon after by Fredrick MVP.

Basketball

Kareem Abdul-Jabbar (1969-1989)

The career points leader, Jabbar is responsible for helping the Lakers finally win something. At 7'2", his skyhook was basically impossible to defend, which led to his 72 straight wins in high school, his three college championships, and his six NBA championships. Jabbar converted to Islam and is often called "one of the good ones."

Charles Barkley (1984-2000)

Though Barkley never won a championship, he led the Philadelphia 76ers, Phoenix Suns, and Houston Rockets to a great deal of playoff losses. One of the most dominant power forwards to ever play, "The Round Mound of Rebound" was known for a sense of humor. Hopefully other athletes reading this book have one, too.

Elgin Baylor (1958-1972)

Baylor was so bad academically that he had to drop out of high school. But somehow that didn't stop Baylor from being the star forward for two different college teams. The number one overall pick in the 1958 draft, Baylor set numerous scoring records and retired just before the Lakers won a championship.

Larry Bird (1979-1992)

The fifth-highest scorer in NCAA history, Bird also turned the Boston Celtics into a winning team and a three-time NBA champion. Bird was one of the best white guys to ever play basketball and perhaps the ugliest, too. No offense Gheorghe Muresan.

Wilt Chamberlain (1959-1973)

Chaimberlain still holds the NBA record for single-game scoring and single-season points per game, among others. He's most notorious for his claim to have had sex with 20,000 women. Realistically, it's probably around 15,000 at best.

> **Other Milestones In Wilt Chaimberlain's Sexual Career**
>
> 2,000 girls whose name start with M
>
> 4,500 dry humps
>
> 22 nine-somes
>
> 20,000 awkward goodbyes
>
> The world's first ménage-a-eighty

Bob Cousy (1950-1970)

A scrappy point guard, Cousy led his Celtics to five NBA titles in an era before he had to play against black guys. Still, he was pretty good. Cousy still has the record for most free throws in a game with 30, a mark nearly bested by Shaquille O'Neal the game he took 4,000 shots.

Julius Erving (1971-1987)

One of the highest scorers in NBA history, Dr. J was one of the main reasons the ABA wasn't laughed out of the country. Erving is known for creating the above-the-rim style of play, as well as the "Orange Julius" franchise.

Walt Frazier (1967-1980)

Before he became an annoying broadcaster who feels he has to rhyme everything, Frazier led the Knicks to their last two championships. Which were over thirty years ago. But Frazier, yeah, he was good.

John Havlicek (1962-1978)

Winning eight titles with the Boston Celtics and one with Ohio State, Havlicek is one of the best defensive players to ever suit up. He also holds Boston records for points and games played, which is impressive since the Celtics used to be really good.

Magic Johnson (1979-1996)

Part of the 1980s Lakers teams that finally won something, Magic Johnson is most well-known for having HIV. Johnson famously announced that he'd contracted the disease more than ten years ago and somehow still does not have AIDS. He's truly magic.

Michael Jordan (1984-1993, 1995-1998, 2001-2003, 2012)

What a crappy baseball player. Seriously, that guy sucked.

Karl Malone (1985-2004)

With the second most points in NBA history, Malone was also known for his dirty play. It has often been said that the player atop his MVP awards should be elbowing someone. Malone is also the first black guy to be liked by most of Utah.

Moses Malone (1974-1995)

The first player to turn pro out of high school, Malone played for two ABA teams and six NBA teams. He played twenty-one seasons--more than any other player in history-- and was great during the first ten or fifteen of them.

Pete Maravich (1970-1980)

"Pistol Pete" Maravich is the NCAA's all-time leading scorer, averaging 44.2 points per game while playing before the three point line. Maravich averaged 24.2 points over his NBA career, which consisted of very good seasons for pretty crappy teams.

True Fake Stat: **238**

Other basketball players that could have a firearm in their nickname.

George Mikan (1948-1956)

Mikan won seven championships for teams in three leagues and helped redefine basketball to emphasize size. Mikan also played in trademark round glasses, which would get him laughed out of the league today.

Earl Monroe (1967-1980)

Earl "The Pearl" Monroe was known for his ability to surprise defenders with circus shots. Monroe helped the Knicks to their 1973 championship and recently had a team named after him – the Baltimore Pearls. Which is better than the Baltimore Monroes.

> **Other Teams Named For Basketball Players**
>
> Wilt Chamberlain: The Stilts
>
> Karl Malone: The Mailmen
>
> Pete Maravich: The Pistols
>
> David Robinson: The Admirals
>
> Dennis Rodman: The Genital Herpes

Hakeem Olajuwon (1984-2002)

Thanks partly to Michael Jordan's vacation, Olajuwon led the Houston Rockets to two championships. Olajuwon was a true Houston local, having first starred at the University of Houston before his time with the Rockets. Except the whole thing about him being Nigerian.

Shaquille O'Neal (1992-When He Becomes a Cop)

A giant among giants, O'Neal's sheer size helped him become one of the best centers to ever play the game. The only thing as big as Shaq is his mouth; he may have won four NBA championships, but they came from three different teams.

Bob Pettit (1954-1965)

The guy on this list you've probably never heard of, Pettit was the NBA's first MVP and led the St. Louis Hawks to an NBA title. You've probably never heard of them either. But, yeah, they were good.

David Robinson (1989-2003)

Robinson's nice, non-flashy demeanor scared many others in the NBA, but he helped make the Spurs one of the dominant teams in the league. He and Tim Duncan combined to form a duo called "The Twin Towers," which was somehow still their nickname after 2001.

Oscar Robertson (1960-1974)

The only player to average a triple-double for an entire season, Robertson was the catalyst on a Milwaukee Bucks championship team. Robertson was also head of the players union during a suit that stalled the ABA merger, and nicknamed "The Big O." Which now means orgasm but back then it was a simpler time.

Bill Russell (1956-1969)

Russell is a five-time MVP, a twelve-time all-star, and a member of eleven NBA champion Celtic teams. He also won two championships in college and a gold medal in the Olympics because, hey, why not.

Isiah Thomas (1981-1994)

Thomas set the record for assists in a season with the Pistons before he set the record as the most inept GM the Knicks have ever had. Thomas spent much of his career in controversy over his rivalries with better, nicer players. That makes his back-to-back NBA championships seem pretty inconsequential.

Bill Walton (1974-1987)

The leader of a UCLA team that won 88 straight games, Walton won college player of the year three years running. Walton's NBA career was highlighted by an MVP award, a few championships, and 732 trips to the doctor.

Jerry West (1960-1974)

One of the most clutch players in NBA history, West teamed with Elgin Baylor to lead the Lakers to one NBA championship and several playoff losses. West is known for his prolific scoring and for being the NBA logo. You can tell by how white it is.

Football

Sammy Baugh (1937-1952)

Known as the first great quarterback, Baugh led the Redskins to the league championship his rookie season. Baugh is the last surviving charter member of the Pro Football Hall of Fame, unless he dies before you buy this. That would be sad.

Jim Brown (1957-1965)

Sporting News named him the greatest professional football player of all time. Sportswriter Bert Randolph Sugar named him the number one athlete of all time. I say he was terrible in *Mars Attacks*. Either way, Brown was a fantastic football player, and a marginal actor.

Dick Butkus (1965-1973)

If your name was Dick Butkus, you'd become a football player, too. Butkus was known for his fierce tackles, which were fueled by all the teasing he suffered on the playground.

Worse Names For Your Son Than Dick Butkus

Pat Manasses

Otto Beagirl

Prostate McGee

Peggy Fleming

Clopton Wingfield

The Los Angeles Angels of Anaheim

Earl Campbell (1978-1985)

A Heisman winner, first overall draft pick, and league MVP, Campbell was also a decent football player. In 1980, Campbell led the Oilers and the league with a staggering 1,934 yards and 373 carries. Partially because he was the only player on the Oilers at the time.

John Elway (1983-1998)

The only quarterback to have started five Super Bowls, John Elway is Denver Broncos football. Except when they suck, then that's someone else's fault. Most people forget that Elway's storied career started with a selfish trade demand and a bunch of whining, but most people aren't Colts fans.

Brett Favre (1991-Forever)

Jeez, is this guy still playing? Favre has been the backbone of the Green Bay Packers since his rookie year in 1732. He's the only three-time league MVP, and won all three consecutively. He also retired years ago, even though he's still playing.

Otto Graham (1950-1955)

A world class tailback in college, Graham was drafted by the Detroit Lions. But before he played professional football, he managed to serve in the Navy and win a basketball championship for the NBL's Rochester Royals. He finally signed with the Browns, where he became one of the best quarterbacks of all time. How did he do all that? Maybe there were just fewer athletes back then.

Red Grange (1925-1934)

Nicknamed "The Galloping Ghost," Grange was the first big college player to help professional football capture the attention of America. Grange developed his strength at an off-season job hauling ice, which is totally what players still have to do.

Joe Greene (1969-1981)

A ten-time Pro Bowler and the core of the Steelers' Steel Curtain defense, Greene is best known for a Coke commercial. As opposed to Darryl Strawberry, who is best known for doing coke.

Don Hutson (1935-1945)

The first star wide receiver in NFL history, Huston is credited with creating many of the pass routes used today. He was also the Green Bay Packers' kicker and a great safety. There really didn't used to be many athletes.

Deacon Jones (1961-1974)

The man who invented the sack, Jones was nicknamed "The Secretary of Defense" for his eerie resemblance to Donald Rumsfeld. Jones missed just six games in fourteen seasons, and we're hoping one day he tackles Rumsfeld.

Bob Lilly (1961-1974)

A defensive force on the Cowboys, Lilly won a Super Bowl and played in 11 Pro Bowls. His 29-yard sack of Bob Griese is one of the most memorable plays in football history, second only to Janet Jackson's half boob.

Dan Marino (1983-1999)

The greatest quarterback to never win a Super Bowl, Marino set just about every passing record there is. Including being the best quarterback to never win a Super Bowl.

Joe Montana (1979-1994)

A four-time Super Bowl winner, Joe Montana led the 49ers to greatness and the Chiefs to slightly less mediocrity. In four Super Bowl appearances, Montana never threw an interception or lost a fumble. Did you read that, Rex Grossman?

Joe Namath (1965-1977)

Namath is the only bright spot the New York Jets have ever had. He won Super Bowl III after guaranteeing he would, despite probably being drunk at the time. And he really wants to kiss Suzy Kolber.

Ernie Nevers (1926-1931)

Never heard of Nevers? That's because he made his name as a Duluth Eskimo and a Chicago Cardinal. Nevers once scored six touchdowns in one game while kicking the extra points, too. He also gave up two of Babe Ruth's 60 home runs in 1927. Really – Nevers also pitched. Eat it, Bo Jackson.

Walter Payton (1975-1987)

Until recently, Payton held the NFL record for rushing yards. He led the Bears to a Super Bowl win and starred in "The Super Bowl Shuffle." You win some, you lose some.

Jerry Rice (1985-2004)

A wide receiver for 21 seasons, Jerry Rice holds the NFL records for touchdowns, touchdown receptions, all-purpose yards, receiving yards, receptions, and a billion other things I don't have room to list. Rice also set the record for most pathetic exit by a great player when he played for three other teams and then competed on two reality shows. Hey, Jerry, maybe you could convince the Real World to shoot in San Francisco again.

True Fake Stat: 0

Times it's ever a good idea for a superstar ex-athlete to go on a reality show.

Barry Sanders (1989-1998)

Sanders retired at the height of his career, falling just short of Walter Payton's then-rushing record. Many wonder why he left the game so soon, but football fans know that Sanders left to retain the use of his knees and to stop having to play for the Lions.

O.J. Simpson (1969-1979)

O.J. Simpson swears he never played professional football. But if he did, he would have played for the Bills and become a prolific rusher. If he did it.

Emmitt Smith (1990-2004)

The NFL's all-time leading rusher, Smith helped the Cowboys to three Super Bowls along with Troy Aikman and a pile of cocaine shaped like Michael Irvin.

Lawrence Taylor (1981-1993)

A force for the New York Giants, Taylor was so dominant at linebacker that he changed the way many teams ran their offense. He also did more cocaine than Michael Irvin.

Jim Thorpe (1920-1928)

The only pure athlete to not be compared to Jim Thorpe, Thorpe excelled at many sports. Playing three seasons for the baseball Giants and barnstorming a bit as a basketball player, Thorpe excelled most at football. But he was a Native American so most white people hated him.

Jim Thorpe's Indian Names

Running Jim

Shooting Jim

Hitting Jim

Catching Jim

Messes With Whitey

Johnny Unitas (1956-1973)

Drafted in the 19th round and released by the Pittsburgh Steelers, Unitas was forced to work construction to support his family. Then he signed with the Colts and became one of the best quarterbacks ever. Good call, Steelers.

Reggie White (1985-2000)

White recorded a then-record 198 sacks during his career with the Green Bay Packers and Carolina Panthers. But White is best remembered for uttering comments so racist that he lived up to his last name. White also appeared in anti-gay newspaper ads, angering every gay football fan. Both of them.

Hockey

Jean Beliveau (1950-1971)

Eventually playing parts of 20 seasons with the Montreal Canadiens, Beliveau didn't want to play professional hockey at first. But Beliveau was so good that the Canadiens actually bought a league and turned it pro in order to exercise a loophole in Beliveau's contract. Beliveau reluctantly played professional hockey, instead of playing for the Rangers.

Ray Bourque (1979-2001)

The record holder for most goals, assists, and points by a defenseman, Borque played 21 seasons with the Boston Bruins before they let him go to a good team and win a Stanley Cup.

Mike Bossy (1977-1987)

Winning four Stanley Cups with the Islanders, Bossy was one of the best snipers the game has ever seen. He also sniped other players verbally, even attacking Wayne Gretzky through the press. He probably had a few choice words for Mother Theresa, too.

Martin Brodeur (1991-He Decides To Stop)

On pace to shatter most goalie records, Brodeur has been to the playoffs all but one of his thirteen seasons with the Devils. Brodeur was a rookie for the Devils when they lost to the New York Rangers, en route to the Rangers' Stanley Cup. Odd phrase, I know.

Bobby Clarke (1969-1984)

Clarke won two Stanley Cups and three MVPs with the Flyers. He later became a general manager and picked up a knack for losing the Stanley Cup, doing so four times. He was also named General Manager of a Canadian Olympic hockey team that didn't win a medal. So really he should have stuck with the player thing.

Phil Esposito (1963-1981)

Esposito was so good at tipping in goals, fans bought bumper stickers that said, "Jesus saves, Espo scores on the rebound." Esposito set many scoring records, all of which have been shattered by Wayne Gretzky. But before that Esposito was seen as really good.

Wayne Gretzky (1979-1999)

Perhaps the most dominant athlete any sport has ever seen, Gretzky is simply known as the Great One, and you'd know that if you paid attention during the hockey chapter.

True Fake Stat: 5

Athletes that have unsuccessfully tried to nickname themselves "The Great One."

Doug Harvey (1947-1969)

Harvey set the standard for defensemen, playing for the dominant Montreal Canadien teams of the 1950s. Harvey was also an outspoken critic of the NHL's low salaries, which is why he was punished by being traded to the Rangers.

Dominik Hasek (1991-2002, 2003-Whenever)

Nicknamed "The Dominator" for dominance in the goal and sexual tastes, Hasek has played for four NHL teams. He retired five years ago even though he is still playing. Look it up.

Gordie Howe (1946-1971, 1979-1980)

Nicknamed "Mr. Hockey," Howe's dominance is second only to his pugilism. Howe even has an official statistic names for him: a Gordie Howe hat-trick involves scoring a goal, getting an assist, and winning a fight. Two franchises actually keep track of that. Howe also once dated Ms. Krabappel.

Edna Krabappel's Other Dates

Principal Seymour Skinner

A TV Dinner

Phil Esposito

Bobby Hull (1957-1980)

Playing 23 years of professional hockey, Hull broke the single-season goal record, becoming the first player to ever score more than 50 goals in a season. Just about everyone has done it since, but back then it was a big deal.

Jaromir Jagr (1990-He Gets Too Old)

The youngest player to ever score in a Stanley Cup at 19, Jagr has been a force almost twenty years. Okay, so he sucked when he was on the Capitals, but aside from that he's been really good.

Newsy Lalonde (1917-1927)

Aside from allowing me to write about a guy named "Newsy," Lalonde was one of the first great hockey players, scoring in the first ever NHL game (and the next five, too). A multi-sport athlete, he was also lacrosse's first great star. And probably lacrosse's only great star.

Guy Lafleur (1971-1985, 1988-1991)

Winning five Stanley Cups and pronouncing his first name "G-ee," Lafleur led the league in scoring three times. He's also the toughest guy to ever be nicknamed "The Flower." And perhaps the only straight guy.

Mario Lemieux (1984-Cancer, 2000-2006)

Lemieux saved the Penguins twice, as the best player in franchise history and as the guy who bought them out of bankruptcy in 1999. Despite tendonitis, a herniated disc, cancer, and playing in Pittsburg, Lemieux is arguably the second best offensive player of all time. Mike Bossy is still more offensive.

Mark Messier (1979-2004)

Having played twenty-five years in the NHL, Mark Messier finally retired in 2004. Messier was seen as the catalyst that finally got the Rangers their Stanley Cup. So to Ranger fans, Messier is Jesus. Even to Jewish Ranger fans.

Stan Mikita (1958-1980)

Probably the best center of the 1960s, Mikita came to Canada as a young boy to avoid communism and pay 90 cents on the dollar. He started as a bit of a goon, but stopped fighting later in his career to become both a gentleman and Canadian.

Howie Morenz (1923-1937)

Considered by many old timers to be the best player in history, he's considered statistically to be eh. Morenz's quickness and electrifying play made hockey tolerable to many fans.

Bobby Orr (1966-1979)

Signed by the Boston Bruins at age 12, Orr is responsible for the turnaround that saw the Bruins reach the playoffs 29 straight seasons. I'm unsure who is responsible for them sucking ever since.

Maurice Richard (1942-1960)

Richard was the original Rocket; he started playing in 1942, when Roger Clemens was just a boy. Richard won eight Stanley Cups and was the original player to score 50 goals in 50 games. He was thankfully never brought to the ice by Elton John's "Rocketman."

Jacques Plante (1952-1973)

Plante was the first goalie to stop the puck behind the net, the first goalie to raise his arm during an icing call, and the first goalie to be named Jacques Plante. He also standardized the goalie mask, which makes me wonder what the hell the other guys were doing not wearing masks.

Patrick Roy (1984-2003)

Probably the top goalie of all time, his name unfortunately falls alphabetically after Plante. He holds the record for career wins, playoff wins, games played, and playoff games played. And his name is pronounced, "wha?"

Terry Sawchuk (1949-1970)

Another goalie in alphabetical order? This is absurd. Anyway, Sawchuck won rookie of the year in three different leagues, and he was pretty good after that, too. He won four Stanley Cups and remains the NHL's shutout leader. In fairness, he played against the Rangers a good deal.

Eddie Shore (1927-1940)

The NHL's first goon, Shore set a record for penalty minutes in his first season. Marty McSorely shattered that in his first game, but you get the idea. Shore is a four-time MVP, and could also beat the crap out of you.

Steve Yzerman (1983-2006)

The longest serving captain of any team in NHL history, "Stevie Y" led Detroit to three Stanley Cups. He's in the top ten in goals, assists, points, and names starting with "Yz." Canadians are weird.

Mohammed Ali (1960-1981, Boxing)

Probably the best boxer ever, Ali became as well known for his trash-talking as he was for his speed and ability. Refusing to fight in the Vietnam War, Ali lost the ability to box for a few years. The draft-dodging Ali was eventually allowed to fight again when the Supreme Court reversed the decision, citing the precedent of Bush v. Kerry.

Mario Andretti (1968-1982, Car Racing)

With 109 major circuit wins and four IndyCar titles, Andretti is the only driver to have ever won the Indy 500, Daytona 500, and the Formula One championship. Mario's son Michael also won the IndyCar title in 1991. His other son, Jeff, is a disappointment.

Eddie Arcaro (1932-1962, Horse Racing)

The only rider ever to win the Triple Crown twice, Arcaro has won more American Classic Races than any other jockey in history. He's tied for the most Kentucky Derby wins with five, and has the most wins at the Preakness and Belmont with six each. Arcaro passed away in 1997, and his cremated ashes were laid to rest in an engraved thimble.

Lance Armstrong (1992-2005, Cycling)

Lance Armstrong is perhaps the most amazing athlete, period. Not only did he win the Tour de France a record seven times in a row, but he did it after recovering from cancer and willingly listening to Sheryl Crow. His "Livestrong" bracelets raised tens of millions of dollars for cancer research, and inspired millions of young people to wear other, more annoying bracelets.

David Beckham (1992-A Few Years From Now, Soccer)

The only Englishman to score in three World Cups, Beckham is one of the most decorated soccer players of all time. Partly because he's incredibly good and partly because he's dreamy. He also married a Spice Girl, which is cool since most of us just masturbated to them.

True Fake Stat: 11

How attractive David Beckham and Posh Spice's children will eventually rank on a scale of 1-10.

Bonnie Blair (1988, 1992, 1994, Speed Skating)

Winning five gold medals and one bronze, Blair has won more Winter Olympic medals than any other United States athlete. Mainly because we suck at the Winter Olympics.

Bjorn Borg (1973-1984, 1991-1993, Tennis)

Winning just under 90% of all the Grand Slam matches he ever played, Borg dominated tennis more than anyone. He is also the only decent tennis player to ever be named "Bjorn." Assuming we're not counting Martina's older sister, Bjorn Navratilova.

Other Famous Bjorns

Anna Bjornikova

Bjorenthal James Simpson

President George W. Bjorn

Don Budge (1933-1954, Tennis)

Budge was the first Grand Slam winner, and held the number one ranking for five years. He was known for his backhand, which he practiced on the help when his tea was served too cold.

Dick Button (Figure Skating)

A five-time world champion and two-time Olympic gold medalist, Button was the first American world champ, first American Olympic skating medalist, first to land a double axel, and first to land a triple jump. He got the name "Dick" because it's short for Richard, not because you are what you eat.

Julio Cesar Chavez (1980-2005, Boxing)

Chavez won six world titles and finished with a record of 104-5-2. He was such a dominant fighter that a Mexican labor leader was named for him.

Nadia Comaneci (1976, 1980, Gymnastics)

The first gymnast to be awarded a perfect ten, Comaneci was one of the few Russians that Americans didn't hate. She won five gold medals, three silvers, and a bronze in just two Olympics. I wonder if the bronze is currently being used as a paperweight or a doorstop.

Jack Dempsey (1914-1927, Boxing)

Okay, so Cesar Chavez is not named for Julio Cesar Chavez. But there's actually a fish named for Jack Dempsey. Dempsey was the World Heavyweight Champion from 1919-1926 and was known for being colorful and aggressive. Hence the fish.

Dale Earnhardt (1979-2001, Car Racing)

His seven championships tie him with Richard Petty for most in NASCAR history, and the league ranked him second on their list of all-time greatest drivers. He won 76 races in his career, and would have won more had he not lost a crucial lap to a cement wall. Oh, I'm going to get hate mail for that one.

George Foreman (1969-1997)

Foreman regained the heavyweight title in 1994 –twenty years after he first held it. That made him the oldest (and perhaps fattest) man to ever win it. Partially because Butterbean never got a title shot. Foreman was also the first boxer to invent a grill, which we all thank him for on a daily basis.

A.J. Foyt (1956-1992, Car Racing)

Probably the best all around driver, he won races in just about every possible category, and is a member of four different racing Hall of Fames. One of those is the National Midget Auto Racing Hall of Fame, even though Foyt himself was not a midget.

Carlos Gracida (1970-Current, Polo)

Gracida is Polo's only Grand Slam winner, and he's done it three times. The closest any other polo player has gotten to a Grand Slam is at Denny's.

Steffi Graf (1982-1999, Tennis)

With 22 career Grand Slam events, Graf is the winningest tennis player of all time. She not only won the Grand Slam in 1988, she also won an Olympic Gold that year. That makes her the only player to ever win "The Golden Slam" because it was made up in 1988 to accommodate her.

Scott Hamilton (1984, Figure Skating)

A four-time world champion, Hamilton also owns an Olympic Gold. He's most well known for his affinity for Dick... Button.

Mia Hamm (1991-2004, Soccer)

Hamm has scored more international goals in her career than any other player, male or female. She owns a share of three Olympic medals, four college championships, and two World Cups. She also won the WUSA championship, which would mean more if the league hadn't folded so quickly.

Sonja Henie (1928, 1932, 1936, Figure Skating)

Henie won more Olympic medals and World Championships than any other figure skater, and was a great actress as well. Kind of like Tonya Harding, if Harding ever won any medals.

True Fake Stat: 411

Times Sonja Henie would have been called "Sonja Heinie" if she went to 8th grade in America.

Eric Heiden (1980, Speed Skating)

In 1980, Heiden won an unprecedented five gold medals by taking all five speed skating events. Amazing, since most people get bored by speedskating after the first few races.

Ben Hogan (1929-1971, Golf)

In 1953, Hogan won five of the six major tournaments he entered, including the first three of the year. More impressively, he did all that after a near fatal car accident that left him almost paralyzed. And he walked twenty miles to school in a snowstorm.

Evander Holyfield (1984-Any Day Now, Boxing)

Holyfield was in a ton of historic fights, and he'll tell you about them once he regains his ability to form sentences.

Jack Johnson (1894-1938, Boxing)

The first black heavyweight champion, Jack Johnson won the title in 1908 and spent the next seven years defending his title by beating the hell out of white guys. If you were him, you'd have done it, too.

Bobby Jones (1916-1930, Golf)

Jones was so good that he retired when he was 28 and still ranks as one of the best golfers of all time. Still the only golfer to win the Grand Slam in one year, I wonder how many tournaments Jones could have won had he not retired early. Like, say, fifty years early.

Jackie Joyner-Kersee (1984, 1988, 1992, 1996, Track & Field)

The winner of three gold, one silver, and two bronze medals, Joyner-Kersee is one of the top heptathletes of all time. Which does not mean she is an athlete with hepatitis, although that's what it sounds like.

Gary Kasparov (1985-2005, Chess)

Kasparov was the world's number one chess player for about twenty years, which is a long time to be number one at anything. Even something as simple and non-strategic as chess.

> **Other Things Gary Kasparov Is Better At Than You**
>
> Sudoku
>
> Matching paints at the Home Depot
>
> K-Turns
>
> Maintaining an eBay business

Billie Jean King (1968-1983, Tennis)

Though she won a combined 28 singles and doubles Grand Slam titles, King is most famous for her participation in the battle of the sexes. King proved once and for all that a female tennis player in her prime can beat a 55-year-old man. Take that, society!

Greg LeMond (1981-1992, Cycling)

America's first winner of the Tour de France, LeMond won the race three times. He then spent the rest of his life criticizing Lance Armstrong.

Carl Lewis (1984, 1988, 1992, 1996, Track & Field)

Named "Olympian of the Century" by *Sports Illustrated*, Lewis won nine gold medals and one silver over an amazing 12-year Olympic career. One of those gold medals is being held from Ben Johnson in an elaborate game of "keep-away."

Greg Louganis (1976, 1984, 1988, Diving)

Winning four Olympic golds and one silver, Louganis is best known for being gay. Because America is terrified of gay people.

Joe Louis (1934-1951, Boxing)

With a record 25 successful title defenses, Louis is the only man who can truly give Ali a run at the title of the greatest fighter of all time. Louis held the heavyweight title for almost twelve years until he finally retired in 1949, giving way to a young George Foreman.

Magnus (Strongman)

I'm not even sure which Magnus, because all the Strongmen seem to be named Magnus. I once saw a guy carry a rock in the shape of Africa really far.

Diego Maradonna (1976-1997, Soccer)

Living proof that cocaine and soccer can mix beautifully, the walking 8-ball was voted FIFA's best player of the 20th century. He led Argentina to the 1986 World Cup, where Maradonna scored almost as many times as Madonna.

Rocky Marciano (1947-1955, Boxing)

Okay, so Marciano could also give Ali a run for his money. Marciano is the only fighter to retire without even tying, having won all 49 of his fights. He won 43 of them by knockout, too. He and his wife Adrian now reside in Philadelphia, not too far from a great deal of steps.

Edwin Moses (1976, 1984, 1988, Track & Field)

Probably the best hurdler of all time, Moses won 122 consecutive races and set the world record in his event four times. Moses is also known for his great reforms in the world of drug testing, which seem to be working ever so well.

Martina Navratilova (1975-2006, Tennis)

Tennis experts agree that Navratilova is one of the two greatest female tennis players in history. That puts her in a pair of women, which she'd totally dig.

Jack Nicklaus (1961-Eventual Death, Golf)

Holding the record for most majors and most senior tournaments won, Nicklaus is the one guy people say is still better than Tiger Woods. But as a kid, I often confused him with Jack Nicholson.

Jesse Owens (1936, Track & Field)

Winning four gold medals in one Olympics doesn't seem too important now, but consider that Owens was black and it was 1936 Germany. Owens' startling performance against the Germans proved Hitler's Aryan Race theory wrong, and helped Americans hate black people a bit less. Briefly.

True Fake Stat: 0

Germans rooting for Jesse Owens at the 1936 Olympics.

Arnold Palmer (1954-2006, Golf)

Golf's first popular star, Palmer utilized television in an era when golf was generally considered very boring. You know, the 20th century. Palmer has a drink named for him, which is the most exciting thing to ever happen around golf.

Pele (1956-1977, Soccer)

More impressive than Pele's obvious greatness is his tireless efforts to help the poor. When Pele scored his 1000th goal, he dedicated it to the poor children of Brazil. The children thanked him and promptly cut up the ball and ate it, with each child getting one of the little hexagons.

Things Poor Kids, While Appreciative, Would Rather Get Than a Soccer Dedication

Food
Shelter
Clothes
Nintendo Wii

Richard Petty (1958-1992, Car Racing)

NASCAR's greatest driver (take that, Dale Earnhart!), Petty won a record 200 races in his career including 27 in one season. No one could turn left better than Richard Petty.

Mary Lou Retton (1984, Gymnastics)

The first gymnast outside of Eastern Europe to win the all-around Olympic title, the American Retton won five medals at the 1984 Olympics. Granted, most of Eastern Europe boycotted that particular Olympics but that's still awesome.

Sugar Ray Robinson (1940-1965, Boxing)

Probably the best pound-for-pound boxer of all time, Robinson is only not considered the best because he wasn't a heavyweight. He was, however, a welterweight champion and a record five-time middleweight champion. Which means he lost it five times, too, but there's no need for a semantic argument.

Ronaldo (1993-Someone Shoots Him, Soccer)

Leading Brazil to the 1994 and 2002 World Cups, Ronaldo is one of the greatest living soccer players. Because you can hardly call what Diego Maradonna does "living."

Pete Sampras (1988-2002, Tennis)

Sampras won a record 14 career men's Grand Slam events, but more importantly, he's married to uber-hottie Bridgette Wilson. That's the grandest slam there is.

Secretariat (1973, Horse Racing)

A horse? If ESPN can include him, so can I. ESPN listed Secretariat as the 35th greatest athlete of the 20th Century, narrowly edging out Oscar Roberston. In 1973, the horse was the first to win the Triple Crown in twenty-five years. Secretariat went on to sire over 600 horses, narrowly edging out Sean Kemp.

Willie Shoemaker (1949-1990, Horse Racing)

Winning 11 Triple Crown races and 8,833 overall, Shoemaker held the record for most career victories for almost thirty years. In tribute to Shoemaker, I'm leaving this entry short.

Mark Spitz (1968, 1972, Swimming)

Holding the record for most gold medals in one Olympics (seven), Spitz won a total eleven medals in his career. He set 33 world records, including being the first Jewish athlete to be that damned good.

Mike Tyson (1985-2005, Boxing)

Mike, if you're reading this (or more likely someone is reading it to you), I love you and please don't eat me.

Tiger Woods (1996-He Gets Bored, Golf)

The guy responsible for making golf bearable, Woods has been named AP Male Athlete of the year four times and was the highest paid professional athlete in 2005. Which is insane because he's a freaking golfer. Woods also has the record for most weeks at the number one spot and holds records at all four grand slam events. This paragraph was presented to you by Nike.

Babe Didrikson Zaharias (1938-1956, Golf)

Probably the best female athlete ever, Didrikson was an Olympic medalist in javelin, hurdles, and high jump – and her basketball team won an AAU championship. But she decided to give up athleticism for golf, where she won 17 amateur titles and even competed in a men's PGA event. Also, she wasn't a lesbian.

CHAPTER TEN

10

Sometimes, sports figures become known for something other than their feats on the field. For instance, Barry Bonds probably has shriveled steroid balls. Just saying. (This time, the year they became infamous will be in parenthesis, like this sentence.)

Baseball

Albert "Don't Call Me Joey" Belle (1994)

It's not just that he destroyed his friends' property, the clubhouse, and women, but he may have done it all with a corked bat. Belle, one of the meanest sluggers to ever slug, is well-known for his time with the Indians and White Sox, as well as with local authorities.

Barry Bonds (2001)

Hi, I'm Barry Bonds. I was on pace to be one of the greats. But I took enough steroids to kill all the cattle in Texas anyway. I have a giant melon for a head.

Bill Buckner (1986)

Buckner is the best example of how one crucial error can erase an entire career. A former batting champ who retired two decent seasons shy of 3,000 hits, Buckner will always be remembered for an error that gave the Mets Game Six of the 1986 World Series. Thank you, Bill. Thank you.

Al Campanis (1987)

While GM of the Dodgers, Campanis went on Nightline and said that black players lacked the ability to become managers, and "don't have the buoyancy" to be swimmers. He also said goodbye to his job two days later.

Jose Canseco (2005)

Jose Canseco hit three career home runs. His steroids hit another 459. It's hard to dislike Canseco as he's one of the only honest players when it comes to taking performance enhancers. Also, he boned Madonna and that's kind of cool.

True Fake Stat: .373

Jose Canseco's BAWBM
(Batting Average While Boning Madonna).

Charles Comiskey (1919)

The owner of the Chicago White Sox, Comiskey is the man behind the Black Sox Scandal. The team actually got the nickname a year before they threw the World Series because Comiskey was so cheap he wouldn't pay for laundry more than once a week. Really.

Steve Howe (1984)

I shouldn't make fun of Howe. Everybody deserves a second chance.

Mike Kekich & Fritz Peterson (1973)

Two Yankee pitchers, Peterson and Kekich actually swapped families. Wives, kids, dogs, everything. This was not a reality show or a publicity stunt, it was just crazy. Peterson ended up marrying Kekich's former wife and having four kids, though Kekich didn't last with his new, um, bride? Possibly the most bizarre moment in baseball, the Kekich/Peterson trade will go down as the worst trade in Yankee history. Even worse than Jay Buhner for Ken Phelps.

Julio Machado (1991)

While at home in Venezuela for the off-season, Machado shot and killed a woman. He's been in Venezuela ever since.

Juan Marichal (1965)

Marishal is the only Hall of Fame pitcher to hit an opposing catcher with a bat. John Roseboro needed 14 stitches to fix the crease in his head and Marichal got a paltry nine-game suspension. Probably because he wasn't gambling at the time he hit Roseboro.

Denny McLain

The last major leaguer to win 30 games, McLain managed to land in prison for racketeering with the Gotti family. One of his arrests even came while he was already in prison on other charges. At least authorities didn't have to look very far to find him.

John Rocker (2000)

In an interview with *Sports Illustrated*, Braves closer John Rocker trashed everyone from black people to gay people to Asian people to New Yorkers to people with AIDS. Rocker subsequently broke down from all the media attention and was out of baseball in a few years. He now lives in Atlanta with his wife, a gay black Asian New Yorker with AIDS.

Who Else Does John Rocker Hate?

The Left-Handed

Redheads

People Named Carl

Tall women

The Staff of *Sports Illustrated*

Pete Rose (1989)

Pete Rose will make the Hall of Fame eventually. You can bet on it.

Marge Schott (1993)

While owner of the Cincinnati Reds, Schott made a number of bizarre comments, most notably that Hitler started out okay at first but then he went too far. The same would later be said about Schott.

Darryl Strawberry (1995)

Maybe he just did all that cocaine because his nose was kind of big and he needed more than the average guy.

Ugueth Urbina (2005)

Once one of the top closers in baseball, Urbina is now in a Venezuelan prison for using gasoline and pitchforks to try and kill five ranch workers. Maybe he can pitch against Julio Machado in the Venezuelan penal league all-star game.

Basketball

Ron Artest (2004)

Artest set the record for flagrant fouls in a season and then broke it the following year. The main guy at the center of the Pistons/Pacers brawl, Artest makes hockey goons look innocent. Artest is also a fledgling rapper, and probably has more street cred than most.

Len Bias (1986)

When the Celtics picked him #2 in the NBA draft, Bias must have celebrated with a cocaine binge. Because that's what he died of two days later. Since the tragic event, Bias's death has been used to promote a drug-free NBA, which is going swimmingly.

Kobe Bryant (2003)

Kobe probably didn't rape the girl who accused him of it in Colorado. But at the very least he cheated on his wife with a gold-digging idiot. Which is pretty commonplace in the NBA, but still it was a big story.

Carlton Dotson (2003)

Baylor basketballer Carlton Dotson is in prison for murdering his teammate and friend Patrick Dennehy. Though they probably weren't very close after the murder thing.

Bobby Knight (2000)

One of the winningest coaches in college basketball history, Bobby Knight is also known for throwing chairs, choking players, and wearing an offensively bright red sweater. He coached Indiana University until they got fed up with him. Or until he threatened his boss, I forgot which came first.

Dennis Rodman (1994)

One of the best rebounders ever, Rodman also rebounded from a wrestling career, cross-dressing, and Madonna. There's an old adage that says when you have sex with someone, you're having sex with everyone they've ever had sex with. Assuming that's true, Dennis Rodman has had sex with Jose Canseco.

Latrell Sprewell (1997)

Sprewell did more in his career than just choke coach PJ Carlesimo for 10-15 seconds. Sprewell also came back 20 minutes later and swung at the guy.

Kermit Washington (1977)

During a brawl, Washington punched Rudy Tomjanovich so hard that Tomjanovich was leaking spinal fluid into his mouth. I never said this chapter would be pretty. Tomjanovich was actually knocked ahead into 1994, where he coached the Rockets to an NBA championship.

Jayson Williams (2004)

Williams shot and killed a limo driver at his estate, probably accidentally. But who twirls a loaded gun while giving a tour of the house? No, Jayson, I don't need the full tour – I'll just wait 'til you guys get back. The foyer is just fine.

Lyle Alzado (1992)

The first athlete to admit to steroid use, Alzado died of brain cancer at 42. Before his death, he blamed the illness on the growth hormones he took, which were harvested from corpses. Ew.

Rae Carruth (1999)

I don't really see the problem. Anyone who has ever thought about preventing their pregnant ex-girlfriend from suing for child support has hired hit men to kill her while escaping in the trunk of a car.

Mark Chmura (2000)

In 1997, Green Bay Packer Mark Chmura refused to meet president Clinton during a Super Bowl celebration because of the Monica Lewinsky scandal. Which made things even funnier when the married Chmura had sex with the 17-year-old babysitter of his children at a post-prom party. The incident was ironically like the Lewinsky scandal. Close, but no cigar.

True Fake Stat: **0**

Funnier examples of karma than Mark Chmura.

Maurice Clarett (2006)

One of the best college football players in the country as a freshman in 2002, the Ohio State running back saw his life unravel when he accepted money, failed out of school, and filed a phony insurance report. After unsuccessfully suing for the right to enter the draft early, Clarrett was eventually drafted by the Denver Broncos, only to rob a few people, run from the cops, and finally be stopped with an arsenal in his car. While being arrested, Clarett allegedly shouted, "don't you know who I used to be!"

Jimmy "The Greek" Snyder (1988)

The Greek was fired from his job as a CBS football commentator after comments that blacks were superior athletes because they were bred that way during slavery. CBS apologized, stating that Snyder acted that way because he was bred to be racist and ignorant.

Woody Hayes (1978)

A longtime Ohio State coach, Hayes is best known for his boxing ability. He attacked a cameraman in 1956, a reporter in 1959, and a player in 1978. He also charged a few people in between, but never connected so it's no big deal. If only Hayes was around Columbus for Maurice Clarett, maybe the coach could have beaten some sense into him.

Michael Irvin (1996)

Part of the Cowboy's Super Bowl teams of the 1990s, Irvin was the main reason the Cowboys were known as South America's team. Irvin's repeated drug arrests did stop him from playing a complete 1996 season, but it didn't stop him from getting a job at ESPN as a commentator. He's thankfully no longer with ESPN, which leaves him free to pursue other opportunities. Like at a network in Colombia.

Fred Lane (2000)

The 2000 Carolina Panthers were really a dream team. Lane, a teammate of Carruth's, was suspended for violating the league's drug policy. While suspended, he was murdered by his wife so he wouldn't squeal on her for her bank robbery. Go Panthers!

Ryan Leaf (1998)

A second overall pick for San Diego, Leaf's 1 for 15, four-yard and two-interception performance stands as one of the worst games in NFL history. And it's a career highlight. After fighting with reporters, fans, and an utter inability to complete a pass to anyone in a Chargers uniform, Leaf was gone. A few attempted comebacks later, and he was out of football completely. 1998's number one overall pick Peyton Manning just won a Super Bowl. Good call, Colts.

10 Jobs Ryan Leaf Has Held Since Retiring

Despite an initial hesitance to sign up for the draft, Leaf began a career as a Marine. He went AWOL one week later, allegedly due to his aversion to powerful arms.

A few moths later, Leaf turned up in St. Louis with a beer distributorship. On his first day, Leaf wigged out and destroyed the entire place when a customer asked him if he carried any Colt.

Leaf then moved to Washington D.C., where he clerked for a civil court judge. All went smoothly until the first trial, when Leaf knocked the judge to the floor, and claimed the bench for himself.

Leaf moved to Oregon, where he tried to turn his love for nature into a new career. He joined an animal rescue campaign, but got fired after the yearly audit. Leaf's boss discovered he had kept

$525,000 that was previously earmarked to save a group of sea hawks.

Leaf's accounting glitches at the nature preserve merited him a job as a financial advisor to Martha Stewart. But after examining his track record, Stewart cut him. "I'm supposed to listen to a guy who turned a $11.5 million signing bonus into a league minimum salary in three years?" Stewart said. "Forget that. Is Mary Meeker available?"

Living with his parents, Leaf took up odd jobs around the house, earning fifty cents at a time. Though his mother was happy to help him get back on his feet, Leaf couldn't seem to stay there.

Turning up at a McDonalds in Dayton, Leaf held his own as a fry-cook for an hour. When patrons began complaining that their meal wasn't satisfying, Leaf first blamed the check-out counter, then the guy at the drive-thru, and finally his manager, before quitting in disgust.

Leaf next tried to mount a Kurt-Warner-style comeback by bagging groceries in the Save-Mart in Sioux City, Iowa. He was dismissed after continually putting groceries on the opposing shelves.

Showing an artistic side, Leaf unveiled his latest art at a SoHo gallery. Critics were angered; while they expected to find masterpieces, the artist formerly known as prospect provided them with bust after bust.

Distraught, Leaf finally returned to football, this time as a coach for a small high school in Great Falls, Montana. Leaf was excited about the season, until a run-in with a hot-headed quarterback forced him into retirement. "I can't stand this," Leaf said, before storming out of a locker room one last time. "Kid thinks he knows it all. Maybe he'll head off to some big school and star there. And draw national attention, perhaps rated one of the best quarterbacks in the country. And then he could even be a number two overall pick. But then what? This kid has got no future."

Ray Lewis (2000)

After a Super Bowl party, Lewis was arrested with two friends for the stabbing death of two others outside of a night club. Lewis swore he wasn't there when it happened--until he was offered a plea bargain. Then he saw everything. The NFL didn't punish him, unless you count winning the Super Bowl MVP a year later as punishment.

Todd Marinovich (1992)

While Marinovich was in high school, a *Sports Illustrated* article discussed how Marinovich was raised by his former NFL dad to be the perfect quarterback, even going as far as keeping him away from fast food. Ironic, since that's probably all Marinovich ate when he was constantly high. Add paternity suits and rape charges to the drug abuse and you've got a bit less than the perfect quarterback.

Randy Moss (1997-2007)

The prototypical goon, Moss has done everything from drugs to hitting a police officer with his car to saying that the plane crash that wiped out the Marshall football team "wasn't nothing big." Just typical stuff, really.

Randy Moss' Training Regimen

Action: Lost a college scholarship over beating up a high school classmate.

Reason: The phrase "one man to beat" means a lot to a wide receiver.

Action: Kicked off the team and jailed one month for marijuana use.

Reason: When you're as fast as Moss, smoking the defense is part of your game.

Action:	Fined for "excessive verbal abuse" of a side judge.
Reason:	Moss was just practicing his trash talk for the league's cornerbacks.
Action:	Squirted a field judge with a water bottle.
Reason:	When you win a Super Bowl, someone is going to need to know how to dump the Gatorade.
Action:	Grabbed a field judge's arm.
Reason:	He was trying to role-play, seeing what it's like committing offensive pass interference.
Action:	Fined for twirling in the end zone after a touch down.
Reason:	Receivers constantly have to spin away from the defense. You should always keep your skills sharp.
Action:	Fought with a sponsor over a seat on the team bus.
Reason:	Like any good football player, Moss was protecting his field position.
Action:	Pushed a police officer half a block with his Lexus.
Reason:	Ever hear of bump and run?

Nate Newton (2001)

When you are caught with 213 pounds of marijuana in your van, you should probably not get caught with another 175 pounds a few weeks later. That's exactly what happened to Newton in 2003. The craziest part is that pot is made of leaves – picture how big 386 pounds of leaves would have to be. Everything is bigger in Texas.

> ### Worse Ways to Smuggle Pot Than Through Nate Newton
>
> Burning it.
>
> Throwing it away.
>
> In front of police dogs.
>
> Giving it to Ricky Williams.

Terrell Owens (2003, 2004, 2005, 2006)

Speaking of things being bigger in Texas, Owens is the biggest train wreck to come through the state since the Crash at Crush. Owens, who alienated the 49ers and the Eagles, is well on his way to doing the same with the Cowboys. With barbs at teammates, spitting at opponents, and an alleged suicide attempt, he's a bus accident away from his own *Behind the Music* special.

Lawrence Phillips (2005)

Phillips was one of the best collegiate running backs of all time – success that didn't translate into the NFL. Possibly because Phillips was too busy beating up women. Having beaten several ex-girlfriends, Phillips also drove his car into a few teenagers for dessert. He now faces twenty years in prison, and I'm not even sure for which incident.

Barret Robbins (2003)

Robbins missed the Super Bowl after he mixed alcohol (a depressant) with his own manic depression, and was cut from the team a year later for steroid use. Most bizarre, a policeman had to shoot him three times during a 2005 brawl in Miami. Why three times? Because when you shoot a guy in the chest twice and he's still coming at you, you shoot him again.

Darrell Russell (2002)

Banned from the NFL for his seventh infraction of the league's drug policy and accused of videotaping the rape of a drugged woman, Russell may have gotten off easy when he was killed in a car crash.

O.J. Simpson (1994)

What a great golfer.

Hockey

Todd Bertuzzi (2004)

Angry at Colorado's Steve Moore for a cheap shot to a teammate three weeks beforehand, Vancouver enforcer Todd Bertuzzi followed Moore down the ice late in the third period. Bertuzzi ended up punching Moore from behind while dragging him to the ice, fracturing three vertebrae in Moore's neck. Moore also received a concussion, vertebral ligament damage, stretching of the bronchial plexus nerves, and a pretty cut up face. Moore hasn't played since, and Bertuzzi played in the Olympics. Seems fair.

Mike Danton (2004)

A rookie left winger, Danton was arrested for trying to hire a hit man to kill his agent. His agent happened to be David Frost, who was later charged with 12 counts of sexual exploitation on three females and four males ages 14 to 16. Did Frost abuse Danton? We'll never know. But if Danton was looking to avoid sexual exploitation, prison is not the best place to do that.

Steve Durbano (1983)

Aside from being one of hockey's villains on the ice, Durbano also had a few extracurricular activities after retirement. Most notable was his attempt to import half a million dollars of cocaine into the US. There was also the shoplifting and running an escort service thing, but the cocaine was probably the biggest.

Dany Heatly (2003)

Nothing is worse than injuring yourself in a car accident induced by speeding and boozing, unless you also kill your friend. That's what Heatly did when the car he was driving hit a wall and killed teammate Dan Snyder. Heatly is now doing quite well, scoring over 100 points last season. Snyder isn't doing quite as well.

Wayne Maki (1969)

In a preseason game, Maki and "Terrible" Ted Green had a bit of a fight. Which is normal in hockey, except for the part where they were swinging their sticks. Green suffered a fractured skull and a brain injury, so I guess Maki won.

Marty McSorley (2000)

At least hockey's violence comes on the ice. In the final seconds of a game that was clearly over, McSorley took a two-handed swing at Donald Brashear's head, knocking him unconscious. McSorley was suspended for the rest of the season, and following an assault conviction he was suspended for the following year. It was the end of McSorely's playing career, though he has appeared in movies and TV shows like Bad Boys, Con Air, and CSI: Miami. Hmm – what do those all have in common?

Bob Probert (1989)

How does a hockey enforcer become a hockey enforcer? Probert, known as the most brutal enforcer of all time, got his moxy from drugs. While in the league, he was arrested for smuggling cocaine across the border and spent three months in a federal prison. In and out of rehab, Probert's problems have extended well into retirement. Today, he can not enter a bar or cross the border without an immigration waiver. Might I suggest a new legal term: Probertion?

Other Sports

Andres Escobar (1994, Soccer)

During the World Cup, Colombia's Escobar accidentally deflected the ball into his own net, giving the US team a surprise victory and Escobar two weeks to live. When Escobar was murdered, the killer shouted "goooooooooooooal!" for each of the 12 bullets. Escobar didn't make it to the 1998 Cup.

Tonya Harding (1994, Figure Skating)

What a bitch.

Ben Johnson (1988, Track & Field)

A Canadian defeating Carl Lewis for Olympic gold was an improbability, but that's what happened. Briefly, anyway

– Johnson's gold was stripped after he tested positive for steroids three days later. USA! USA!

Floyd Landis (2006, Cycling)

Speaking of drugs stripping things, American Floyd Landis' recent Tour de France victory was heralded as an amazing comeback – until Landis tested positive for three times the legal limit of testosterone. Landis alleged that he just has a lot of that stuff naturally. Sure – and Ben Johnson was drugged. Canada! Canada!

Marie-Reine Le Gougne (2002, Figure Skating)

A judge of the pair skating competition in the Olympics, the French Le Gougne judged the Russian pair much higher than they should have been, and some sort of treachery was suspected. Turns out it was part of a deal with the Russians to let the French win the ice dancing competition. We know that because when Le Gougne was confronted, she broke down crying in the lobby of her hotel. That's right – the French judge immediately surrendered.

Panama Lewis (1983, Boxing)

Lewis found a solution to his fighter Luis Resto being the underdog. Lewis removed the padding from Resto's gloves, and Resto won. Temporarily – the state boxing commission found out about Lewis's actions, and both Lewis and Resto were charged with criminal possession of a weapon, conspiracy, and tampering with a sports contest. Lewis was banned from boxing for life and sentenced to six years in prison. Where he thankfully knew how to box.

Claudine Longet (1976, Skiing)

Longet was the actress who infamously shot and killed skier/boyfriend Spider Sabich. Longet claimed Sabich's gun accidentally went off when he was showing it to her. Which explains why he was shot in the back from six feet away.

Mike Nifong (2006, Lacrosse)

Nifong is the least athletic on the list, as the prosecutor of the Duke lacrosse rape scandal. Using the scandal to elevate his career as district attorney, Nifong led the witch hunt against the three students. At the time of publication, all three were cleared of the charges and Nifong is now being investigated by the North Carolina Bar Association. Possibly because six months into the national news frenzy, he admitted having never even talked to the alleged victim about the case. He'll have plenty of time to catch up with her after he's disbarred.

> **What Mike Nifong Will Do After He Gets Disbarred**
>
> Cry.
>
> Drink.
>
> Hire a stripper.

Gunter Parche (1993, Tennis)

After Monica Seles supplanted Steffi Graf as the top woman on the tennis circuit in 1993, Graf supporter Gunter Parche stabbed Seles in the back. Graf quickly became the number one tennis player again, and Tonya Harding got an idea.

Bill Tilden (1946, Tennis)

How do you top a career as one of the best tennis players of all time? Why, with a teenage male prostitute and seven months in prison, of course. And how do you top that? By trying to have sex with a 16-year-old male hitchhiker and ten more months in prison. Despite being born wealthy and being a big earner on the tennis circuit, the pedophile died broke after spending most of his money financing Broadway flops that he wrote, starred in, and produced. Might I recommend a new one called "15-Love."

Mike Tyson (1991, Boxing)

Beyond biting an opponent twice, raping a girl, assaulting motorists, beating Robin Givens, DUI, assaulting reporters, cheating on his wife, drugs, squandering a $300 million fortune, and advocating eating babies, what has Mike Tyson really done wrong?

CHAPTER ELEVEN

Why Do Hot Dogs Cost Four Dollars?
(Get it? It's called "chapter eleven.")

Whose Fault Is It, Anyway?

Baseball is the most inexpensive of the major sports, mainly because of the size of the stadiums and number of games. For a baseball team to sell out, they'd need to sell approximately four million tickets. For a hockey team to sell out, they'd need to sell a quarter of that. Which is still challenging, since no one cares about hockey.

Even the cheapest of the major sports, baseball is still incredibly expensive. A decent ticket costs $25. That's $100 for a family of four. Add hot dogs, soda, a program, parking, and a souvenir official team licensed piece of garbage, and you're up to almost $200 to attend a game. For $200, you can do a lot of things – like buy a computer, a week's worth of groceries, or even half a tank of gas. So I can understand why some fans would rather stay home. Unfortunately, most of us do not.

Teams charge a ton for games, merchandise, and hot dogs because fans are willing to pay for it. Sports is a business first and a hobby third. Because it is also a business second.

How Did This Happen?

In the beginning of most sports, there was a strong push to keep them amateur. But pretty quickly, owners and promoters realized that there was money to be made and a business was born. There is no such thing as amateur athletics anymore. Even little leaguers are playing for the chance to become professionals. Little League is the summer internship of the sports world.

Even adult leagues, filled with aging fat guys who are way past their prime (assuming they ever had a prime), usually have prizes. Or at the very least, bragging rights. Show me someone who plays competitively just for the love of the game and I'll show you someone who owns a time machine.

But even once most sports turned professional, it took a while before player salaries and ticket prices got out of control. Mainly because it took a while for the owners to let it happen.

Putting the "Own" in Owner

Owners used to be called owners because they owned both the team and the individual players that made up the team. But within just a hundred or so years of that system being set up, players finally rebelled and got a say in where they play and who they play for. Most players exercise that say just about every year, but it took a while to get there.

The era of a player spending his career with one team is over, except for players that get kicked out of the league after one season. Now, players change teams as often as teams change colors and stadiums change names, making the whole thing very confusing. If leagues could think long-term, there'd be a league-sponsored bonus to any player who re-signs with his original team. Of course, if leagues could think long-term there'd have never been a Fox Puck.

True Fake Stat: **Several**
People who should apologize for the Fox Puck.

Television – Nature's Banker

When television first started trying to broadcast baseball games, owners shied away from the idea because owners are stupid. Also because radio didn't bring in the kind of revenue that TV eventually offered. No one has ever heard of a $100 million dollar radio deal. Except Howard Stern.

Now that TV has become the central part of the sports landscape, any sport or league that can get TV time earns a great boost. Sports fans can now watch paintball, rock-paper-scissors, and scrabble before writing angry letters to the network for airing that crap. TV has redefined sports, and not just through exposure. Not the Steve Lyons type exposure, either.

TV has changed sports so much that many leagues build in commercial breaks to the structure of their games. And new sports build their presentation around television, like the sponsorships professional poker players wear. Hey, if scrabble is a sport, so is poker.

We Reap What We Sow

There is a myth that you don't truly support your team unless everything you own supports your team. MLB's old school baseball bed sheets are tame compared to NASCAR's new line of meat products. If the PGA released an oxygen tank, we could officially eat, sleep, and breathe sports.

Twenty years ago, baseball cards cost 40 cents a pack and came with 17. Now a pack of 10 costs three dollars. Yes, I sound a bit like an old man telling you the bus used to cost a nickel, but the point is that baseball cards have gone up by more by ten times their price. Think gas is expensive? Topps' Finest makes a Humvee seem affordable.

And as we continue to pay higher prices, the prices will continue to rise. Good luck getting a decent throwback jersey for under $200. Aside from at a garage sale. The only way to stop this madness is to stop paying for it. But then what kind of fan would you be?

CHAPTER TWELVE

What Comes Next? (Just Bust a Move)

Trends

There are several trends in sports, some of which I might even include in this book. I will probably write a section for them called "trends" and place it in, say, chapter twelve.

Sponsorship

When Comiskey Park became U.S. Cellular Field in 2003, everyone realized that millions of dollars were worth far more than nostalgia. There are now only a few stadiums just named for teams, like Angel Stadium. Which is more commonly known as Los Angeles Angel Stadium of Anaheim in California of Los Angelesly's Anaheimness. Pretty soon, every stadium and arena will be named for a bank, except Wrigley Field. Which will continue to be named for chewing gum.

Sections of games are becoming sponsored as well. Half-time shows & highlights already feature sponsors, and it won't be long before every pitch, pass, and traveling call will have an endorsement. If refs ever called traveling. The website of the

Hagerstown Suns (Class A affiliate of the Washington Nationals) offers the opportunity to sponsor the first pitch, the call to the bullpen, and strikeouts. The one thing you can't sponsor is their ability to contribute to a quality major league team.

Uniforms are not sacred either. Newer sports like NASCAR, poker, and paintball are swamped with sponsors, who actually believe those three things are sports. Even sports like football and basketball already feature somebody's logo, and that's just going to grow. And if you think the older sports are safe, ask the Hagerstown Suns how much it costs to sponsor batting practice jerseys. I'm surprised that the list on their website doesn't include a menu.

Television Restructuring

As television's influence on sports increases, the structure of the games will continue to change. We've already seen the TV timeout, but stay tuned for games that start in line with the fall schedule, and product placement during games.

"He's going back, back, back, leaping at the wall! He got it! What an amazing great catch. I was so surprised I almost spilled my Coke. Mmmm, coke. The pause that refreshes."

Coke, if you're reading this, I'd appreciate a few bucks for that plug.

Internet Restructuring

Television is no longer new media – it's being supplanted by the internet. And as video on the internet grows, so will sports coverage. The only problem is that internet video is usually limited to a few minutes, so expect sports to follow suit. By 2010, YouTube will broadcast the first internet Olympics, featuring one event with one competitor. Maybe it will be a footrace and we'll come full circle. The United States will still find a way to lose.

Niche Sports

With more and more choices of cable channels, television ratings are going down quickly. There's simply more to do now, so one specific game doesn't earn the ratings it used to. Sports TV found an answer – niche programming.

Paintball, Spelling Bees, and Rock-Paper-Scissors have all found their way onto TV. Are they successful? Sure. If just the families of the participants watch, that's better ratings than some other channel's "Who Wants to Be a Furniture Builder?" reality show. I bet some programming executive is reading this right now and thinking, "Who Wants to Be a Furniture Builder? That WOULD make a good show."

How Major League Baseball Can Become the National Pastime Again

- Team mascots available for birthday parties.
- 30 randomly selected fans now earn the league minimum.
- Every day is bobblehead day.
- Randy Johnson made available to reach things on high shelves.
- Seventh-inning stretch cheerleaders.
- Anti-trust exemptions for everyone!
- Three words: Pepper games allowed.
- While his team is in the field, designated hitter combs the stands picking up trash.
- Every time your team wins, the manager takes you out for ice cream.
- When your team is on the road, the stadium will be available for beer league softball games.
- Stadium organ players take requests.

Zero Tolerance Three-Strike Policy

The more athletes get in trouble, the more sports are allegedly cracking down. Nothing sends a clear message like a huge suspension that can and will be appealed shortly thereafter. Leagues will eventually formulate a "zero-tolerance three-strike policy," where athletes only get three chances to get a fake suspension before receiving an even longer fake suspension. And after that, it's time for a double secret fake suspension. Unless the athlete is really good, in which case he can do what he wants.

Goodbye, Steroids

Eventually, the sports pendulum will swing back and it will become cool not to be on steroids. Instead, athletes will return to the good old days, when guys were just boozing and paying for sex like all good role models.

True Fake Stat: 95%
People who are seen as innocent and take steroids.

True Fake Stat: 100%
People who are named Barry Bonds and take steroids.

Equipment Improvements for Sports Writers

The Writer's Facemask: No one wants to be poked in the eye with their own pen. Now, writers won't fear asking tough questions since their eye sockets will be protected. Comes in three styles: Catcher, Goalie, and Tiki Barber.

Boxer Varnish:

Cover all exposed skin with the varnish. If any boxer tries to bite you, he will learn his lesson when he gets a mouth full of the stuff.

Sideline Kneepads:

Kissing up is hard work, and sometimes people can get sore. Thanks to new Sideline Kneepads, reporters who enjoy the fine art of butt-smooching can go on for hours. Pads can be purchased in red, blue, and Jim Gray.

The Arm Guard:

To prevent ornery interview subjects from getting testy and knocking the mic out of a reporter's hand. However, users should be careful of getting hit by pitches while wearing it.

The Armed Guard:

For anyone interviewing an Indiana Pacer.

Can I Be an Athlete?

Sure you can! There are many sports to choose from, and while each takes a lifetime of commitment and preparation, it will all be worth it when you're banging hot chicks. Especially if you play in the WNBA. Each sport, of course, has a few basics. Here's how to get started.

Soccer:

Learn Spanish.

Golf:

Have rich parents.

Boxing:

Have poor parents.

Gymnastics:

Grow boobs. But really tiny ones.

Basketball:

Be aggressive. B-E aggressive.

Paintball:

Celebrate your 25th birthday with a job at a video store.

NASCAR:

Turn left.

Baseball:

Start playing when you're three, and develop a curveball by age 10. Don't learn a thing in school other than the infield fly; spend your time practicing pickoffs instead. Devote every waking minute of your life to the game so when you get there, you'll be ready. Then, take steroids.

True Fake Stat: A gazillion
Copies of this book you will buy for friends.